OSAT
Mild-Moderate Disabilities
Practice Questions

Mometrix
TEST PREPARATION

DEAR FUTURE EXAM SUCCESS STORY

First of all, **THANK YOU** for purchasing Mometrix study materials!

Second, congratulations! You are one of the few determined test-takers who are committed to doing whatever it takes to excel on your exam. **You have come to the right place.** We developed these practice tests with one goal in mind: to deliver you the best possible approximation of the questions you will see on test day.

Standardized testing is one of the biggest obstacles on your road to success, which only increases the importance of doing well in the high-pressure, high-stakes environment of test day. Your results on this test could have a significant impact on your future, and these practice tests will give you the repetitions you need to build your familiarity and confidence with the test content and format to help you achieve your full potential on test day.

Your success is our success

We would love to hear from you! If you would like to share the story of your exam success or if you have any questions or comments in regard to our products, please contact us at **800-673-8175** or **support@mometrix.com**.

Thanks again for your business and we wish you continued success!

Sincerely,
The Mometrix Test Preparation Team

Copyright © 2023 by Mometrix Media LLC. All rights reserved.
Written and edited by the Mometrix Exam Secrets Test Prep Team
Printed in the United States of America

TABLE OF CONTENTS

- PRACTICE TEST #1 _____ 1
- ANSWER KEY AND EXPLANATIONS _____ 24
- PRACTICE TEST #2 _____ 53
- ANSWER KEY AND EXPLANATIONS _____ 76
- THANK YOU _____ 105

Practice Test #1

1. Mary is a 10-year-old student who has a developmental disability due to a physical impairment. Why would she not be eligible for special education services as a student with a developmental delay?
   a. The developmental delay category does not include physical impairments.
   b. The developmental delay category does not include students older than age 9.
   c. The developmental delay category does not include students with developmental disabilities.
   d. The developmental delay category does not include students younger than age 12.

2. Which of the following is the best example of how the results of an adaptive behavior scale can drive instruction?
   a. To determine which behaviors the students need to work on
   b. To determine whether or not a student needs a behavior plan
   c. To determine which independent living skills a student needs to work on
   d. To determine how to adapt the curriculum to a student's needs

3. Which one of the following education service providers gives instructional assistance to students who receive special education services?
   a. Teaching assistants
   b. Paraprofessionals
   c. Student teachers
   d. Behavior support professionals

4. Max is a fourth-grade student with a visual impairment. Which of the following would be most appropriate in supplementing his math curriculum?
   a. Reading the problems to him orally
   b. Allowing him extra time to work
   c. Providing opportunities for hands-on experiences
   d. Allowing him to use a computer

5. According to IDEA, when would it be appropriate for a due process to occur with regard to a student's IEP?
   a. When the parents disagree with the decisions of the IEP team
   b. When a student needs additional accommodations
   c. When the parents request an evaluation
   d. When a student no longer requires special education services

6. Carter is a sixth-grade student with an intellectual disability. Why would the use of manipulatives be an appropriate instructional strategy when teaching a math lesson?
   a. Manipulatives can stimulate the sense of touch in students with intellectual disabilities.
   b. Manipulatives can serve as visual aids for students with intellectual disabilities.
   c. Manipulatives can help students with intellectual disabilities learn classroom rules.
   d. Manipulatives can aid in communication for students with intellectual disabilities.

7. Jerry is an eighth grader with multiple disabilities. Why would it be beneficial for a teacher to construct a new test to assess Jerry rather than using standardized testing data?
   a. Students with multiple disabilities do not take standardized tests.
   b. Standardized data likely do not assess what Jerry has learned.
   c. Accommodations are not allowed on standardized tests.
   d. Jerry will not need standardized testing data for college admittance.

8. Courtney is an eighth-grade student with a specific learning disability who is at risk due to her use of drugs and alcohol in her home. Which of the following interventions would likely be most beneficial in helping Courtney focus on school?
   a. Offering to meet with her and her parents
   b. Offering to take her to rehabilitation
   c. Offering to refer her to a counselor
   d. Offering to keep her secret safe

9. Which of the following instructional strategies would be most appropriate when teaching a science lesson to a third-grade class?
   a. Reciprocal teaching
   b. Socratic questioning
   c. Direct instruction
   d. Learning centers

10. Joseph is a fourth-grade student being evaluated for special education services as a student with a specific learning disability in the area of math problem solving. Which of the following would be the best interpretation of his assessment results that show he is within one standard deviation of the mean in math problem solving?
    a. Joseph would likely be determined eligible for special education services.
    b. Joseph would likely need more testing in order to determine his eligibility.
    c. Joseph would likely be determined ineligible for special education services.
    d. Joseph would likely be determined eligible for a 504 plan instead.

11. When interpreting the results of a norm-referenced test, how are the scores determined?
    a. By comparing a student's score to a previous score
    b. By comparing a student's score to other students that are the same age
    c. By comparing a student's score to a standard deviation
    d. By comparing a student's score to other students with disabilities

12. Which of the following is true about learned helplessness and students with disabilities?
    a. Students with disabilities typically do not suffer from learned helplessness.
    b. Students with disabilities often learn to control situations.
    c. Students with disabilities tend to reach out for help before they get to learned helplessness.
    d. Students with disabilities often feel like they have no control.

13. Jason is a second-grade student with an intellectual disability. Which of the following characteristics would you most expect to impact his educational performance?
    a. Significantly subaverage general intellectual functioning
    b. Concomitant impairments that cause severe educational needs
    c. Disorder in one or more of the basic psychological processes
    d. An injury to the brain caused by an external force

14. Which of the following is true of the Family Educational Rights and Privacy Act with regard to students who receive special education services?
    a. These protections also apply to private schools.
    b. The school cannot release records without parental consent.
    c. Parents do not have the right to request educational records.
    d. Parental rights belong to the student when they turn 18.

15. When teaching a new group of students, which one of the following strategies is most productive in creating a supportive classroom environment?
    a. Including community-building activities
    b. Allowing the students to negotiate
    c. Posting student work in the room
    d. Establishing authority as the teacher

16. Which of the following was one of the main purposes of the Individuals with Disabilities Education Act (IDEA) of 2004?
    a. To provide opportunities for students with disabilities to learn
    b. To protect the rights of students with disabilities
    c. To afford students with disabilities protection from expulsion
    d. To initiate new programming for students with disabilities

17. Emma is a nonverbal student who is assigned an oral presentation in her history class. Which of the following alternatives best allows her to access the curriculum?
    a. Allowing Emma to present a slideshow instead
    b. Allowing Emma to skip this assignment
    c. Allowing Emma's aide to present the information
    d. Allowing Emma to write a paper on a similar topic

18. Which instructional strategy would be most beneficial in working with a small group of seventh graders who struggle with math calculations?
    a. Using worksheets
    b. Using flash cards
    c. Using visual aids
    d. Using group projects

19. Which of the following is the best example of a postsecondary transition goal for a student who wants to be a veterinarian?
    a. Jimmy will go to college to study veterinary medicine.
    b. Jimmy will research the job requirements of a veterinarian.
    c. Jimmy will become a veterinarian.
    d. Jimmy will take classes in high school to prepare him to become a veterinarian.

20. Disabilities can have an impact on society in many ways. Which of the following factors tends to be most important in determining whether or not a person with a disability makes a positive or negative impact on society?
    a. The type of disability that the person has
    b. The personality of the individual with the disability
    c. The meaning of the disability to the individual
    d. The support system that the individual has

21. Which of the following is not one of the purposes of the prereferral process when evaluating students for special education services?
    a. To evaluate student strengths and weaknesses
    b. To put accommodations and interventions into place
    c. To evaluate accommodations and interventions
    d. To obtain consent to begin the evaluation process

22. Why might it be difficult to incorporate different kinds of activities each day when teaching a class with students of varying disabilities?
    a. Some students require structure in their daily routine.
    b. Some students may not have the knowledge required for each activity.
    c. Some students may not be comfortable working with other students.
    d. Some students require only certain activities in their IEPs.

23. Which of the following is the most appropriate example of a student with a disability receiving support from a peer tutor on a subject they are struggling with?
    a. A 2nd-grade student tutoring a 1st-grade student in math
    b. A 12th-grade student tutoring a kindergarten student in reading
    c. A 7th-grade student tutoring an 8th-grade student in science
    d. An 11th-grade student tutoring a 9th-grade student in writing

24. When writing a behavior intervention plan, what is the purpose of preventive strategies?
    a. Identifying the behaviors targeted for reduction or increase
    b. Finding behaviors that serve the same purpose as the unwanted behaviors
    c. Eliminating the triggers or providing access to events
    d. Teaching the individual skills needed to use tools

25. Rachel is a first-grade student who receives occupational therapy due to her struggles with handwriting. Which of the following sections of the IEP would be most likely to state the nature of this therapy?
    a. Present levels
    b. Accommodations
    c. Service delivery
    d. Prior written notice

26. For which group of students would it be most appropriate to implement a functional curriculum at the elementary school level?
    a. Students with intellectual disabilities
    b. Students with specific learning disabilities
    c. Students with speech or language impairments
    d. Students with developmental delays

27. Which of the following is a disadvantage of an externally facilitated IEP meeting?
    a. The discussion can often get off topic.
    b. It can be difficult to resolve conflicts.
    c. It can make certain members feel left out.
    d. It takes more time to prepare.

28. Gordon is an 11th-grade student with an other health impairment and a postsecondary goal of attending college. Which of the following would likely be least productive for Gordon as he seeks to achieve this goal?
    a. Reaching out to colleges in the area to tell them about Gordon
    b. Assisting Gordon in researching colleges he wants to attend
    c. Helping Gordon to discover professions he may be interested in
    d. Providing opportunities for Gordon to practice filling out applications

29. Which of the following would be the most appropriate for a student who was evaluated for special education services and identified as not having a disability?
    a. Referring the student back to general education without accommodations
    b. Referring the student back to general education with accommodations
    c. Referring the student to the 504 team
    d. Referring the student to supports outside of school

30. Which one of the following components is most important in attaining goals that are measurable?
    a. Concrete evidence
    b. Cost analysis
    c. Clarified descriptions
    d. Overarching objectives

31. Which of the following strategies would be least effective in communicating to parents as the new case manager of a student?
    a. Calling them with an introduction
    b. Setting up a meeting to discuss the IEP
    c. Sending home a note for the student to deliver
    d. Meeting them in person when they pick up their child

32. Which of the following is typically the most challenging in identifying a student who is an English learner for special education services?
    a. The disability may or may not be related to language.
    b. The Individualized Education Program (IEP) may not meet their needs.
    c. Special education services may not be beneficial in English.
    d. The student may already miss too much class.

33. Josh is a preschooler who is just starting school for the first time. Which of the following would be atypical social development for a child of his age?
    a. Showing some separation anxiety
    b. Cooperating with other children
    c. Exploring things independently
    d. Wanting to be like his friends

34. Which of the following is the best reason to implement cooperative learning into classrooms with students with disabilities?
    a. Students are more likely to engage in this structure.
    b. Students receive more support in these kinds of classrooms.
    c. Students receive more instruction from teachers with this model.
    d. Students are more likely to meet IEP goals in this environment.

35. When selecting an intervention for a student who struggles with math problem solving, which of the following strategies would be least effective in improving the student's math skills?
    a. Explicit instruction
    b. Teaching vocabulary
    c. Inquiry-based instruction
    d. Graphic organizers

36. Which of the following functional curriculums would be most appropriate in supplementing the curriculum of a 10th-grade English class for students with autism?
    a. Practice reading street signs
    b. Practice reading textbooks
    c. Practice reading computer terms
    d. Practice reading grocery words

37. How can social-emotional assessments guide instruction in the classroom for students who struggle behaviorally?
    a. Having students answer a survey in order to understand what their preferences are
    b. Having parents answer a survey in order to understand what works at home
    c. Having teachers answer a survey in order to understand what caused the poor behaviors
    d. Having psychologists answer a survey in order to understand what the potential behaviors are

38. Which of the following describes the purpose of an intelligence test?
    a. To measure a student's ability to think abstractly
    b. To measure a student's ability to understand spoken language
    c. To measure a student's ability to convey ideas through oral language
    d. To measure a student's ability to retain visual information

39. Alison is a fourth-grade student with a speech-language impairment due to stuttering. Which of the following strategies would be least effective in providing a supportive classroom environment?
    a. Having her skip presentations in which she has to speak
    b. Having her collaborate with students that she is comfortable with
    c. Having her pass when she is called upon in class
    d. Having her sit near the teacher at the front of class

40. Martin is a 12th-grade student with an intellectual disability working on learning to do his own laundry. Which one of the following examples includes maintenance and generalization when working on this skill?
    a. Practicing doing laundry every day at school
    b. Practicing doing laundry once a week at school
    c. Practicing doing laundry every day at the laundromat
    d. Practicing doing laundry once a week at the laundromat

41. Justin is a fourth-grade student who receives special education services as a student with deaf-blindness. Which of the following collaborative approaches would be most effective at the beginning of the new school year?

  a. Giving the general education teacher access to the IEP to review
  b. Allowing the general education teacher to teach the student as they see fit
  c. Asking the district for advice on working with this student
  d. Meeting with the general education teacher to develop a plan

42. Which of the following resulted from the No Child Left Behind Act of 2001 with regard to students receiving special education services?

  a. Schools were held accountable for the performance of students with disabilities.
  b. Schools were to provide extra assistance for students with disabilities.
  c. Schools were to draft IEPs for students with disabilities.
  d. Schools were to provide postsecondary opportunities for students with disabilities.

43. Mike is a ninth-grade student with a specific learning disability in the area of math calculation. Which of the following will likely have the greatest impact on him across his life span?

  a. Establishing a budget for his earnings and bills
  b. Being able to use measurements
  c. Making change when shopping at the store
  d. Being able to make a schedule

44. Why are objectives important for lesson planning when teaching a group of students with deficits in executive functioning?

  a. To provide students the opportunity to plan what they will be learning
  b. To assess students at the end of the lecture
  c. To give students a task to complete during their learning
  d. To keep students focused on one task

45. Which of the following best describes the purpose of the standard score when interpreting assessment data?

  a. To determine how spread out the numbers are
  b. To determine how far a score is from the average
  c. To determine the rank of the score compared to others
  d. To determine the hypothetical range of scores

46. When teaching a group of high school students with disabilities, which of the following strategies can be implemented to ensure that they have a meaningful learning experience in the class?

  a. Offering to help each student outside of class
  b. Getting to know each student in class
  c. Creating experiences on topics that students are interested in
  d. Giving rewards for students with high grades

47. Which of the following best describes the purpose of the present levels of academic achievement section of the IEP?
   a. To describe how the child is performing educationally
   b. To determine the accommodations that the school accesses
   c. To identify which disability category is appropriate
   d. To compare a student's performance to peers

48. How can the interpretation of curriculum-based assessments be valuable in determining the growth of a student?
   a. By comparing the student's score to others in the district
   b. By comparing the student's score to their grade in the class
   c. By comparing the student's score to the average score
   d. By comparing the student's score to their previous scores

49. Brady is a second-grade student working on reading fluency. Which of the following would be the best example for a demonstration of learning at the end of the lesson?
   a. Asking Brady to read a story and answer questions
   b. Asking Brady to listen to a short reading passage
   c. Asking Brady to read a timed short reading passage
   d. Asking Brady to read a list of words with assistance

50. Peyton is a ninth-grade student with a specific learning disability in the area of math problem solving. How can a diagnostic assessment be used to guide instruction in his math class?
   a. Assessing which accommodations he can access
   b. Assessing which math class is most appropriate
   c. Assessing which goals to develop in his IEP
   d. Assessing which modifications need to be made

51. Samuel is a student with a specific learning disability in the area of oral expression. What kind of assessment would be most appropriate in order to evaluate his continued eligibility?
   a. Expressive language
   b. Receptive language
   c. Auditory discrimination
   d. Verbal intelligence

52. Jessica is a fourth-grade student with a specific learning disability in the area of reading comprehension. How might technology be incorporated into a reading lesson plan in order to meet her needs?
   a. Allowing her to research a story on the computer
   b. Allowing her to access to audiobooks
   c. Allowing her to give a presentation instead of a reading
   d. Allowing her to use her phone while she reads

53. Which of the following students would it be most appropriate to conduct a verbal intelligence test on when reevaluating for special education services?
   a. A student with an intellectual disability
   b. A student with a specific learning disability in math
   c. A student with a specific learning disability in writing
   d. A student with a visual impairment

54. Which of the following is true when describing the least restrictive environment of students receiving special education services?
   a. Students must receive special education services if they have an IEP.
   b. Students with disabilities must receive special education services.
   c. Students with disabilities must be taught with their peers as much as possible.
   d. Students must receive special education services in a separate environment.

55. When teaching a small group of students with intellectual disabilities about science, which of the following characteristics of the lesson plan would be the most beneficial to their learning?
   a. Background knowledge
   b. Practical application
   c. Assessment
   d. Independent practice

56. In which one of the following disability categories would you expect to identify more boys for special education services than girls?
   a. Other health impairment
   b. Specific learning disability
   c. Intellectual disability
   d. Deaf-blindness

57. Dylan is a 10th-grade student with a disability who uses a computer to complete the majority of his work. Which of the following strategies would be most effective for a teacher to be involved in Dylan's instruction?
   a. Reading the prompts from his computer to him
   b. Tutoring him each week after school
   c. Reviewing his grade each week
   d. Checking in with him every day

58. Which of the following is the best example of how a lifelong skill can be appropriately implemented into a lesson plan for high school students with disabilities?
   a. Incorporating the stock market into a math lesson for students with Down syndrome
   b. Incorporating newspaper reading into an English lesson for students with ADHD
   c. Incorporating budgeting skills into a math lesson for students with learning disabilities
   d. Incorporating creative writing into an English lesson for students with autism

59. Which of the following would be the greatest disadvantage of co-teaching?
   a. One teacher may teach more than the other.
   b. The teachers may disagree on strategies.
   c. The teachers may not be experts in certain subjects.
   d. One of the teachers may not have much experience.

60. Melissa is an eighth-grade student who receives services as a student with autism spectrum disorder. Which of the following co-occurring conditions is Melissa least likely to suffer from?
   a. Anxiety
   b. Epilepsy
   c. Sleep conditions
   d. Orthopedic impairments

61. Which of the following instructional strategies would be most appropriate in supporting a student with an independent living skills goal of cooking a meal?
   a. Allowing the student to help in the cafeteria by cleaning the kitchen
   b. Allowing the student to shadow workers at a local restaurant
   c. Allowing the student to research ingredients needed to make meals
   d. Allowing the student to use the kitchen to cook her lunch each day

62. Jason is a third-grade student with behavior needs who often runs out of the classroom. Which of these would likely be the most productive first step if Jason ran out of the class?
   a. Run after him
   b. Call the office
   c. Call the police
   d. Call his parents

63. When planning a lesson for a group of students with severe needs working on life skills, which of the following types of practice would be most likely used to ensure that they understand the material?
   a. Guided practice
   b. Collaborative practice
   c. Independent practice
   d. Student-led practice

64. Jake is an 11th-grade student with an intellectual disability. How might an agency outside of school assist Jake in his postsecondary transition?
   a. Having someone from vocational rehabilitation come talk to him at school
   b. Having someone from an independent living agency provide workshops
   c. Having someone from a recreation center help him explore activities
   d. Having someone from an adult education program give him flyers

65. Which of the following is not true with regard to the role of parental participation in the IEP process?
   a. Parents are members of the IEP team.
   b. Parents can call an IEP meeting.
   c. Parents can run an IEP meeting.
   d. Parents can help develop IEP goals.

66. Which of the following would be the responsibility of the school nurse with regard to students who receive special education services?

   a. Serving as the case manager of the IEP
   b. Ensuring that accommodations are put into place
   c. Implementing mental health services
   d. Providing health updates at eligibility meetings

67. Christopher is a student with concerns in the area of academics who scored in the below-average range on an academic achievement test. Which of the following disability categories would Christopher most likely be eligible for?

   a. Speech or language impairment
   b. Other health impairment
   c. Specific learning disability
   d. Cognitive disability

68. Which of the following would be the least appropriate for a special education teacher to use to evaluate the progress of their students on their IEP goals?

   a. Standardized assessment data
   b. Curriculum-based assessments
   c. Classroom observations
   d. End-of-quarter grades

69. How does the Americans with Disabilities Act benefit those students with disabilities that require special education services?

   a. Students with disabilities are allowed accommodations in the classroom.
   b. Students with disabilities have the right to a free appropriate public education (FAPE).
   c. Individuals with disabilities are guaranteed equal opportunities.
   d. Individuals with disabilities must be taught by highly qualified educators.

70. When conducting an assessment in the area of fine motor skills, which of the following activities would be the most important to observe?

   a. Watching a student draw a picture
   b. Watching a student make numbers with their hands
   c. Watching a student throw a ball
   d. Watching a student ride a bike

71. Which of the following characteristics of culture has the greatest impact on the identification of special education students?

   a. The language the student speaks
   b. The content the student has learned
   c. The location the student comes from
   d. The religion the student practices

72. Joseph is a 10th grader with an other health impairment due to anxiety. Which of the following would be the least effective in structuring his classroom environment?

   a. Giving him a pass to leave the class when he feels anxious
   b. Allowing him to take his tests in a separate setting
   c. Breaking down his assignments into pieces
   d. Teaching him stress-reducing activities at the beginning of each class

73. Suzie is a sixth-grade student with a specific learning disability whose parents have little or no involvement and typically do not respond when the school contacts them. Which of the following strategies would be most effective in involving them in the IEP process?
    a. Continuing to reach out to them until they respond
    b. Sending home forms for them to fill out
    c. Offering that they participate in the meeting by phone
    d. Trying to get a hold of a different family member

74. When working with a group of students with emotional disturbances, which of the following would be the best example of a measurable objective?
    a. Measuring how much a student's behavior has improved
    b. Measuring the number of outbursts that a student has
    c. Measuring how well a student interacts with peers
    d. Measuring how much work a student completes

75. Which of the following would not be an example of a diagnostic assessment?
    a. Pretests
    b. Self-assessments
    c. Interviews
    d. Projects

76. Which of the following is true of the "multiple disabilities" category?
    a. Deaf-blindness can be included in the multiple disabilities category.
    b. Orthopedic impairments cannot be included in the multiple disabilities category.
    c. Students with multiple disabilities cannot be accommodated solely for one impairment.
    d. Students with multiple disabilities remain in this category throughout their schooling.

77. Which of the following would be the least productive method for determining how a test at the end of the unit can be used to improve instruction for the next unit?
    a. Identifying which questions the student struggled with
    b. Identifying which students struggled on the test
    c. Identifying which kinds of questions the students asked
    d. Identifying which curriculum to use

78. How might technical education classes in schools contribute to the prevention of at-risk learners with disabilities?
    a. Students might find these classes more meaningful.
    b. Students might find that these classes have better teachers.
    c. Students might find that these classes are shorter.
    d. Students might find that these classes build community.

79. Which of the following is the best example of maintaining a previously learned concept?
    a. Giving students a daily quiz on vocabulary words
    b. Giving students a study guide to practice vocabulary words
    c. Giving students periodic questions on vocabulary words
    d. Giving students a test at the end of the unit on vocabulary words

80. Rachel is a student with a traumatic brain injury in a life skills class working on job interviewing skills. Which of the following would be the most appropriate summative assessment for this unit?
   a. Assigning a paper
   b. Assigning a multiple-choice test
   c. Assigning a presentation
   d. Assigning a mock interview

81. How can state standardized tests be beneficial in determining the proper instruction for students with disabilities?
   a. Using the results of the tests to determine accommodations
   b. Using the results of the tests to determine class placement
   c. Using the results of the tests to determine IEP goals and objectives
   d. Using the results of the tests to determine the least restrictive environment

82. Which one of the following classroom management methods would be least effective when working with a group of students with ADHD due to attention?
   a. Allowing students to help establish guidelines
   b. Providing tangible rewards to students
   c. Recognizing students when they make a comment
   d. Establishing a points system for behavior

83. Hailey is a seventh-grade student who is hearing impaired and is being evaluated using an intelligence test. If the average standard score of the test is 100 and Hailey scored 75, what does this tell us about her intelligence?
   a. Hailey's score falls in the below-average range.
   b. Hailey's score falls in the low-average range.
   c. Hailey's score falls in the mid-average range.
   d. Hailey's score falls in the well-below-average range.

84. Sally is a ninth grader with an other health impairment who is new to her school. Which of the following should the special education teacher prioritize in helping Sally?
   a. Ensuring Sally is on track to graduate high school
   b. Ensuring Sally has all of her school supplies
   c. Ensuring Sally's teachers understand her accommodations
   d. Ensuring Sally's permanent file is up to date

85. Which of the following strategies would be the least productive when working with a disabled student who is suspected to be a victim of abuse?
   a. Listening to the student and trusting what they say
   b. Reporting the incident to child services
   c. Continuing to teach them in the same manner
   d. Asking the child for more details on the incident

86. Typical cognitive development in a child between the ages of 2 and 6 would consist of which of the following?
   a. A child that manipulates objects
   b. A child that uses perception in their thought process
   c. A child that applies logical reasoning
   d. A child that has abstract thoughts

87. Lisa is a fifth-grade student with a disability who will often exhibit defiance in her class. Which of the following would be the best example of a formative assessment in order to evaluate Lisa's behavior?
   a. Asking her to participate in class discussions
   b. Conferring with her throughout the year
   c. Observing her behavior in the class
   d. Allowing her to skip certain lessons

88. Which of the following is a component of the constructivist learning theory?
   a. Student behaviors are shaped by specific actions that lead to specific responses.
   b. Student behaviors are shaped by mental processes that are measured.
   c. Student behaviors are shaped by past experiences and constructs.
   d. Student behaviors are shaped by the growth of a person over a lifetime.

89. Pat is a second-grade student who has been receiving intervention support outside of his general education class for the last six weeks due to difficulties with reading fluency. What steps should the school take if Pat struggles to make progress?
   a. Continue interventions for another six weeks.
   b. Discontinue interventions.
   c. Refer Pat for special education services.
   d. Refer Pat for a 504 plan.

90. Which one of the following federal laws currently governs special education services in the United States?
   a. Section 504 of the Rehabilitation Act
   b. Individuals with Disabilities Education Act
   c. Family Educational Rights and Privacy Act
   d. Americans with Disabilities Act

91. Which of the following conditions would not typically be associated with a student with an emotional disturbance, according to IDEA?
   a. An inability to learn that cannot be explained by intellectual, sensory, or health factors
   b. A disability significantly affecting verbal communication and social interaction
   c. An inability to build or maintain satisfactory interpersonal relationships
   d. A tendency to develop fears associated with school problems

92. Which of the following learning objectives would be considered appropriately challenging for a group of kindergarten students with math deficiencies?
   a. Students will be able to add numbers.
   b. Students will be able to identify numbers.
   c. Students will be able to subtract numbers.
   d. Students will be able to count to 100.

93. Which of the following would be the most effective long-term strategy in maintaining a safe classroom environment?
   a. Showing the students where the exits are
   b. Ensuring that the classroom is clean and orderly
   c. Posting the class rules on the wall
   d. Establishing positive relationships with the students

94. Text-to-speech assistive technology devices are most appropriate for which of the following students?
   a. Students with autism
   b. Students with hearing impairments
   c. Students with dyslexia
   d. Students with multiple disabilities

95. Which of the following is an example of a personal cultural bias that may impact communication with a student or their family?
   a. Hesitating to contact a student's family because of a past encounter with the family
   b. Hesitating to contact a student's family because of an unfamiliarity with their history
   c. Hesitating to contact a student's family because of an experience with a sibling
   d. Hesitating to contact a student's family because of the community that they live in

96. When teaching a ninth-grade student with a learning disability in the area of reading, which one of the following components is the most important to focus on?
   a. Fluency
   b. Vocabulary
   c. Phonics
   d. Comprehension

97. Christina is an 11th-grade student who receives special education services due to an emotional disturbance and has a hard time completing any work due to frustration. When Christina becomes frustrated enough, she tends to lash out verbally to nearby people. Which of the following would be the most appropriate strategy to include in her behavior plan to help her calm down when frustrated and complete her schoolwork?
   a. Teaching her stress management techniques
   b. Allowing her to complete work in a separate setting
   c. Provide rewards for completing work
   d. Giving her choices about what work she does

98. Which of the following is most important in writing nondiscriminatory assessments?
   a. Getting to know the background of each student in the class
   b. Ensuring the inclusion of multicultural questions
   c. Eliminating biases associated with certain topics
   d. Evaluating each student based on their identity

99. Which of the following environmental factors is most likely to have a positive impact on student achievement?
   a. Location of the school
   b. Climate of the school
   c. Populace of the school
   d. Size of the school

100. Which of the following is an example of how Maslow's hierarchy of needs can be applied to motivate students?
   a. Using fear to allow students to find security
   b. Establishing structure to allow students to find self-actualization
   c. Setting goals to allow students to build self-esteem
   d. Providing food as a reward to fulfill basic needs

101. Billy is a fourth-grade student with an intellectual disability. Which of the following living scenarios is most common for students like Billy after they complete their schooling?
   a. Living in an apartment alone
   b. Living in an apartment with others
   c. Living with parents
   d. Living in a residential facility

102. Which of the following would be the best application of the cognitive learning theory in the classroom setting?
   a. Repetitive practice
   b. Research projects
   c. Collaborative learning
   d. Discussions

103. Which of the following is an example of when it would be inappropriate for a student to access the general education curriculum?
   a. When students need additional reading support
   b. When students need to access modifications
   c. When students need a safe environment
   d. When students need a behavior plan

104. When working with a small group of students with emotional disturbances on regulation, which of the following would be the best way to organize the classroom?
   a. A large classroom with room for the students to move around
   b. A small classroom with students sitting at separate desks
   c. An office where students can engage with each other
   d. A small classroom with students sitting at the same table

105. Which of the following methods of recording observations would be most effective in determining how often a behavior occurs?
   a. Time samples
   b. Observation checklists
   c. Narratives
   d. Anecdotal records

106. Which of the following is the best strategy in teaching students with coexisting disabilities?
   a. Teaching to each disability separately
   b. Teaching the student as a whole
   c. Teaching to the needs of the most impacted disability
   d. Teaching to both disabilities at the same time

107. Which of the following strategies would be most productive when differentiating the writing process for a student with a traumatic brain injury?
   a. Allowing the student the use of a computer
   b. Providing review sheets for exams
   c. Reducing distractions on the student's desk
   d. Slowing down the instructional pace

108. Which one of the following strategies is most beneficial in maintaining a safe learning environment?
   a. Teaching at the front of the classroom
   b. Walking around the classroom while teaching
   c. A combination of teaching at the front and walking around
   d. Sitting with the students while teaching

109. Which of the following is a potential limitation of the Positive Behavioral Interventions and Supports system?
   a. The system cannot be implemented school-wide.
   b. The system cannot be implemented for students with IEPs.
   c. The system is often centered around rewards.
   d. The system is often focused on punishment.

110. Which of the following health problems is included in the "other health impairment" disability category?
   a. Asthma
   b. Cerebral palsy
   c. Traumatic brain injury
   d. Perceptual disability

111. Jordan is a sixth-grade student with a traumatic brain injury who struggles with handwriting. Which of the following professionals would likely assist Jordan in improving this skill?
   a. Occupational therapist
   b. Physical therapist
   c. School nurse
   d. Physical education teacher

112. Susan is a third-grade student with autism undergoing a special education evaluation for concerns with her behavior. How can the results of behavior rating scales assist in understanding the instruction that Susan may benefit from?
   a. Asking teachers to fill out forms
   b. Asking teachers to observe Susan in different settings
   c. Asking teachers to interview Susan
   d. Asking teachers to give Susan a written assessment

113. Which of the following differentiated instruction strategies would be least appropriate when working with students with learning disabilities in a general education English class?
   a. Designing multiple activities to support various learning styles
   b. Grouping students by ability to complete assignments
   c. Assessing students through formative assessments
   d. Lowering the expectations for some students

114. Which of the following behaviors would typically be expected of a third-grade student?
   a. Difficulty managing emotions
   b. Difficulty following directions
   c. Difficulty keeping boundaries
   d. Difficulty handling criticism

115. Which of the following is an instructional strategy that is least likely to be effective when working with a group of sixth-grade students with ADHD?
   a. Offering choices to the students
   b. Providing hands-on learning
   c. Providing the students with a challenge
   d. Repeating instructions often

116. When working with students on writing their name in a kindergarten class, which of the following would be the least effective in generalizing this skill?
   a. Asking students to practice in the classroom during free time
   b. Asking students to practice at home with their parents
   c. Asking students to practice when they go to art class
   d. Asking students to practice with their friends

117. Robert is a kindergarten student who is struggling with some of his motor skills. Which of the following is the most concerning struggle for a student of his age?
   a. His inability to type on a keyboard
   b. His inability to tie his shoes
   c. His inability to use scissors
   d. His inability to tie a knot

118. Which of the following would determine a student to be ineligible for special education services as a student with a developmental delay?
   a. A student with a delay in academic development
   b. A student with a delay in social development
   c. A student with a delay in adaptive development
   d. A student with a delay in physical development

119. Which of the following is the goal of implementing a summative assessment?
   a. To evaluate student learning
   b. To determine the appropriate instruction
   c. To monitor student learning
   d. To compare students to a norm

120. Which of the following is the benefit of closure when planning a lesson?
   a. To ensure the students are assessed properly
   b. To ensure the students understand what was learned
   c. To ensure the students can demonstrate their knowledge
   d. To ensure the students understand forthcoming objectives

121. Which of the following strategies would be least productive for a student with a disability who is at risk of dropping out of school?
   a. Assigning a peer to help them with their work
   b. Reducing the number of assignments
   c. Touching base with the student frequently
   d. Writing a contract with the student

122. When would it be most appropriate to conduct a small group for high school students with emotional disturbances to focus on behavior management?
   a. When the students start the school year
   b. When the students start to display negative behavior
   c. When the students receive a behavior plan
   d. When the students' behavior becomes a pattern

123. Which of the following research-based intervention strategies would be most appropriate for a third-grade student who is working on reading fluency?
   a. Multisensory techniques
   b. Metacognitive strategies
   c. Text structuring
   d. Explicit teaching

124. Corey is a third-grade student with a specific learning disability in the area of reading fluency. Which of the following assessments would be most appropriate in determining his eligibility for special education services?
   a. Wechsler Preschool and Primary Scale of Intelligence
   b. Wechsler Individual Achievement Test
   c. Wechsler Intelligence Scale
   d. Wechsler Intelligence Scale for Children

125. Which of the following is true of the extended school year services section of the IEP?
   a. All students with IEPs receive extended school year services.
   b. Extended school year services must be provided at the beginning of the summer.
   c. Extended school year services must be provided before the school year starts.
   d. Some students are not eligible for extended school year services.

126. Which of the following is the most useful skill for a learning objective in a general education setting for seventh-grade students with specific learning disabilities in the area of writing?

   a. Writing sentences
   b. Writing paragraphs
   c. Writing essays
   d. Writing words

127. When teaching pull-out groups of elementary school students, which one of the following is a disadvantage to working with the students one on one rather than in small groups?

   a. Students do not have access to their peers in one-on-one settings.
   b. Students do not have access to the general education curriculum.
   c. Students do not have access to their general education teachers.
   d. Students do not have access to the special education curriculum.

128. Which of the following grouping techniques would likely be least effective when working with a small reading intervention group at an elementary school?

   a. Grouping by ability
   b. Grouping by age
   c. Grouping by disability
   d. Grouping by behavior

129. Which of the following is not typically considered a service delivery model for a special education teacher?

   a. Co-teaching
   b. Pull-out
   c. Push-in
   d. Resource room

130. Kayla is a fifth-grade student with a specific learning disability in the area of math problem solving. At Kayla's annual IEP meeting, which of the following individuals would likely be a member of the IEP team?

   a. School counselor
   b. Science teacher
   c. School psychologist
   d. School social worker

131. Which one of the following instructional strategies allows students to move around the room while still learning?

   a. Embodied learning
   b. Inquiry-based learning
   c. Blended learning
   d. Service learning

132. Sally is a preschool student who seems to be struggling in many areas. Which of the following can be beneficial in determining what kind of instruction would be most appropriate for her?
   a. Intelligence quotient (IQ) assessments
   b. Curriculum-based assessments
   c. Alternate assessments
   d. Developmental assessments

133. Trevor is a fifth-grade student with co-occurring conditions as a student with a specific learning disability and an emotional disturbance. Which of the following is a benefit of identifying Trevor in both of these areas?
   a. Trevor can receive academic and emotional support.
   b. Trevor can be placed in a self-contained classroom.
   c. Trevor can have a behavior plan.
   d. Trevor can be eligible for alternative placement.

134. Which of the following would be the best option in providing a fifth-grade student with a reading comprehension disability access to the curriculum in his reading class?
   a. Modifying the content that the student reads
   b. Accommodating the student by reading to him
   c. Modifying the assignments that the student completes
   d. Accommodating the student by giving him fewer questions

135. George is a sixth-grade student with a specific learning disability in the area of written expression. Which of the following assistive technology devices would likely be least beneficial to George?
   a. Graphic organizers
   b. Proofreading programs
   c. Frequency modulation (FM) listening systems
   d. Word-prediction programs

136. When co-teaching a high school English class, which one of the following instructional strategies is likely to be least effective in ensuring that all students are achieving in the class?
   a. Both teachers teaching as a team
   b. Teaching the students in stations
   c. One teacher instructing while the other supports
   d. Taking turns teaching and planning

137. Javier is a third-grade student who just moved from Mexico and is struggling with the content in his English class. Which of the following is the best reason for not evaluating him for special education services right away?
   a. Students who are English learners are not eligible for special education services.
   b. It is best to wait and see which disability he may have.
   c. It is best to wait and see the nature of his struggles.
   d. New students often take a while to learn a new curriculum.

138. Richard is a fifth-grade student with autism who takes classes in an inclusion setting. Which of the following factors would likely have the greatest social influence on Richard?
   a. Conforming to their beliefs
   b. Complying with their wishes
   c. Changing their identity
   d. Internalizing their behavior

139. When teaching an eighth-grade geography class with multiple students that require additional support personnel inside the class, which is the best strategy in organizing the classroom?
   a. Having rows of desks
   b. Having desk clusters
   c. Having desks in circles
   d. Having long tables

140. Billy is a 10th-grade student with an other health impairment due to his ADHD. When writing a daily objective for his executive functioning skills, which of the following would be most appropriate?
   a. To be able to use a planner independently
   b. To be able to memorize the state capitals
   c. To be able to sit silently without talking
   d. To be able to repeat teacher instructions

141. Greg is a ninth-grade student with Tourette's syndrome who struggles with social skills. Which of the following would be most appropriate when initially implementing an intervention to focus on socializing?
   a. Pull Greg from one of his classes once a day to work on social skills.
   b. Pull Greg from one of his classes once a week to work on social skills.
   c. Implement this intervention into his general education classes.
   d. Implement this intervention into an after-school activity.

142. Which of the following would be the best example of using technology to meet the needs of all kinds of learners?
   a. Giving a slide show presentation
   b. Grouping students to use tablets
   c. Providing audiobooks to each student
   d. Allowing students to use computers for independent research

143. Jadon is a second-grade student with a goal in written expression. Which of the following curriculum-based assessments would be most appropriate in assessing his progress on his written expression goal?
   a. Giving him 10 minutes to write as essay
   b. Giving him 3 minutes to write spelling words
   c. Giving him 3 minutes to write a paragraph
   d. Giving him 1 minute to write a sentence

144. Which of the following would be the most appropriate reason to use a portfolio when assessing students with disabilities?

a. In order to determine what a student knows at the end of a unit
b. In order to determine what a student's areas of interest are
c. In order to determine how much progress a student makes
d. In order to determine how a student compares to their peers

145. Jason is a third-grade student with autism who excels academically but struggles with attention occasionally in the general education setting. Which of the following strategies will be most helpful in ensuring successful inclusion?

a. Placing Jason with the appropriate general education teacher
b. Pulling Jason from the room when he exhibits certain behaviors
c. Teaching Jason behavior strategies in special education
d. Placing a paraprofessional in Jason's class

146. Which of the following is true of the federal safeguards notice required by IDEA with regard to parents of students with disabilities?

a. Schools must provide the families a copy of their rights.
b. Schools must provide access to educational records.
c. Schools must provide a prior written notice.
d. Schools must provide an independent educational evaluation.

147. A calculator would be best categorized as which type of assistive technology?

a. Low tech
b. Mid tech
c. High tech
d. No tech

148. Which of the following would be the best preventive measure when working with a student that struggles with following directions?

a. Modeling how a student follows directions
b. Teaching the rules at the beginning of class
c. Giving the student consequence choices
d. Meeting with the student to discuss the behavior

149. Which of the following best describes when a formative assessment would take place in the classroom?

a. Before the instruction
b. While the students are learning
c. After the learning has been completed
d. At any time during a lesson

150. Which of the following is not true about children with disabilities in foster care?

a. The majority of students in foster care have a disability.
b. The condition of students with disabilities tends to worsen when unplaced.
c. Students in foster care are often victims of abuse.
d. Students with disabilities in foster care can have a difficult time finding placement.

Answer Key and Explanations

1. B: In order to be eligible for the developmental delay category, students must be age 9 or younger. There are many impairments that are included within the category, but students must be a certain age. According to IDEA, a student like Mary would likely be eligible in a different category because of her developmental disability. Answer a is incorrect because the developmental delay category does include students with physical impairments. Answer c is incorrect because students with developmental disabilities such as physical or emotional impairments would be eligible for the category if they meet the age requirements. Answer d is incorrect because students younger than age 10 are included in the category.

2. C: Adaptive behavior scales are used to determine which independent living skills that a student has and what they may need to work on. These assessments are typically used for students with intellectual disabilities or other severe disabilities to understand what instruction needs to be implemented. These tests typically consist of an evaluation of a student's social skills, daily living skills, communication skills, and other skills that they will need after high school. Answer a is incorrect because these scales do not evaluate a student's level of behavior. Answer b is incorrect because the adaptive behavior scale is not used to determine whether or not a student needs a behavior plan. Answer d is incorrect because these scales are not correlated with adapting the curriculum.

3. B: Paraprofessionals provide instructional support to students with disabilities to ensure they have access to the curriculum. Paraprofessionals typically work under the guidance of special education teachers to make sure that students have the accommodations and modifications that they need. These professionals are instrumental in assisting the special education teacher and the general education teacher. Answer a is incorrect because teaching assistants can include a wide variety of people including student assistants or aides for general education classes. Answer c is incorrect because student teachers are typically students who are receiving on-the-job training to become teachers. Answer d is incorrect because behavior support professionals typically work with students outside of school on behavior deficits.

4. C: Although all of these choices can be beneficial in supporting students like Max, it is important to distinguish the difference between accommodations and supplementing his curriculum. Providing opportunities for him to experience hands-on learning can be beneficial in allowing him to feel the numbers and improve his math. Accommodations are tools that allow him to access the same curriculum as his peers. Answer a is incorrect because although reading problems to him orally is beneficial, this is an accommodation to the general education curriculum. Answer b is incorrect because allowing him extra time would not supplement the curriculum. Answer d is incorrect because allowing him to use a computer can be helpful for an alternative curriculum or accommodation but not necessarily to supplement the curriculum.

5. A: A due process can occur when the parents of a student receiving special education services disagree with a portion of or the entire IEP. The parents have a right to challenge the decisions that have been made, and a hearing is held to determine the next actions. It is important for parents to understand that they have these rights if they disagree with the decisions of the IEP team or school district. Answer b is incorrect because if the student needs additional accommodations, the team can amend the IEP. Answer c is incorrect because when the parents request an evaluation, the school must conduct a special education evaluation. Answer d is incorrect because if the student no longer requires services, that student will no longer have an IEP.

6. A: The use of manipulatives in which students get to use their hands can help them learn new concepts, especially in math. Being able to see where objects go and touching the objects allow students with intellectual disabilities to get more involved. Although these students are often visual learners, manipulatives can help in areas such as math and science. Answer b is incorrect because although these students tend to be visual learners, manipulatives can be helpful in stimulating their sense of touch. Answer c is incorrect because manipulatives are not designed to help students learn classroom rules. Answer d is incorrect because manipulatives typically do not help students communicate.

7. B: Although standardized testing data can be valuable for certain students, many students with disabilities are learning an alternate curriculum. Alternative testing is available for some students, but teachers may find that constructing a new test is more beneficial in assessing what a student is capable of. This can be helpful in determining how much progress a student has made over the year or what the student still needs help with. Answer a is incorrect because students with multiple disabilities can still take the standardized tests with accommodations or alternative assessments. Answer c is incorrect because accommodations are typically allowed on standardized tests for students with disabilities. Answer d is incorrect because although Jerry may or may not attend college, standardized data can still be helpful.

8. C: Students can be at risk for many reasons, and drug and alcohol abuse can be one of them. It is important to seek out help for these students while also providing them support at the same time. These kinds of issues must be reported in order to get the students the help they need because of the impact it has on their life and the future. Answer a is incorrect because offering to meet with Courtney's parents might make her think that she is in trouble. Answer b is incorrect because taking her to a rehabilitation facility may be overstepping the boundaries of a teacher. Answer d is incorrect because students who have reported or are suspected of using drugs and alcohol must be reported in order to get them the help they need.

9. D: When teaching a science lesson to a group of third-grade students, it is important to incorporate hands-on learning activities. Learning centers can provide opportunities for these students to do activities and learn about different topics. Learning centers are most appropriate for younger students such as a group of third graders. Answer a is incorrect because reciprocal teaching would be most appropriate for older students who are capable of teaching each other rather than younger students. Answer b is incorrect because Socratic questioning would be most appropriate for higher level questioning based on thoughtful dialogue between the teacher and student and is a skill that third graders likely would not have. Answer c is incorrect because direct instruction may be more appropriate for a more abstract topic such as reading or math.

10. C: When students fall within one standard deviation of the mean, this is most often considered in the average range and a student would not be eligible. Students being evaluated for a specific learning disability must have a score that is considered statistically significant in order to be eligible. It is important to understand where one standard deviation falls in order to determine where the student scores. Answer a is incorrect because the student would likely not be eligible unless they were outside one standard deviation. Answer b is incorrect because although it is possible that more testing could be considered, this score shows that the student is within the average range. Answer d is incorrect because there is likely not enough information to determine whether or not a 504 plan would be appropriate for Joseph.

11. B: Norm-referenced tests can be helpful in that they compare a student's score with a random sample of other students that are of the same age. This allows the evaluator to determine areas of strength and weakness for students by comparing them to others. It is important to understand where the average score stands when interpreting assessment results in order to determine appropriate instruction or programming. Answer a is incorrect because comparing a student's score to a previous score would be considered progress monitoring. Answer c is incorrect because it is important to consider where the standard deviation is when interpreting results, but the score cannot be compared to a standard deviation. Answer d is incorrect because these assessments compare all of the students, not just those with disabilities.

12. D: Students with disabilities often suffer from learned helplessness, or a condition in which they feel like they have no control. These students will often give up because they think that nothing can be done to improve their condition. This is something that impacts individuals with disabilities as they are learning about themselves and what they are able to accomplish. Answer a is incorrect because students with disabilities will often suffer from learned helplessness. Answer b is incorrect because these students with learned helplessness have a difficult time controlling situations. Answer c is incorrect because students with disabilities do not always have the chance to reach out for help before they get to learned helplessness.

13. A: A student with an intellectual disability will have a significantly subaverage general intellectual functioning. This will typically be combined with deficits in adaptive behavior and will be manifested during the developmental period. This is something that likely would be noticed in Jason starting from an early age. Answer b is incorrect because a concomitant, or accompanying, disability would fall under the category of multiple disabilities. Answer c is incorrect because a disorder in basic psychological processes would fall under a specific learning disability. Answer d is incorrect because an injury to the brain by an outside force would be in the "traumatic brain injury" category.

14. D: Parents have the right to access educational records, including IEPs, for students until they turn 18. Once a student turns 18, the parents no longer have the same rights and must request the records through the student. This is important when working with students with IEPs that go to college or transfer to a different school. Answer a is incorrect because these protections do not apply to private schools that do not receive public funding. Answer b is incorrect because there are cases in which the school can release these records without parental consent. Answer c is incorrect because parents do have the right to request educational records within a certain time period.

15. A: Although all of these choices may have their own benefits in helping students feel welcome, community building is likely the best long-term strategy in ensuring that the students feel supported. When students have opportunities to get to know each other and the teacher, they will be more likely to feel welcome and needed. If students do not feel welcome in the class, they may not feel safe and may start to distance themselves from the rest of the class. Answer b is incorrect because if there is too much room to negotiate, the students will not clearly understand the rules. Answer c is incorrect because although posting work in the room can make some students feel welcome and important, other students may be embarrassed. Answer d is incorrect because although it is important to establish authority, it is also important that the students feel like they are involved in the process as well.

16. B: One of the main purposes of IDEA in 2004 was to protect the rights of individuals with disabilities and their families. These laws allowed for parents to be more involved in the special education process and understand and be involved each step of the way. This was important in ensuring that the decisions made were by members of the team rather than just the school. Answer a is incorrect because students with disabilities already had opportunities to learn under previous legislation. Answer c is incorrect because students with disabilities do not have protection from expulsion in most circumstances. Answer d is incorrect because although IDEA may have caused many school districts to implement new programming, it did not specifically call for it.

17. A: Allowing Emma to give a slideshow presentation instead of presenting orally is the best way for her to access the same curriculum as her peers. This way, she is able to prepare and learn the same material as everyone else. Access to the curriculum involves providing opportunities for students with disabilities to learn the same material as their peers. Answer b is incorrect because if she skipped the assignment, she wouldn't gain the knowledge. Answer c is incorrect because having her aide present for her does not provide her with the opportunity to give a presentation. Answer d is incorrect because although she would still learn some of the same material as her peers, she wouldn't get a chance to present.

18. C: Students who struggle with math calculations will likely need an alternative teaching method in order to memorize facts. These students have likely used many of the traditional methods but continue to struggle. The use of visual aids allows students to see the numbers in a different way, which allows them to find a new approach to memorizing these facts. Answer a is incorrect because worksheets do not provide these students with an opportunity to practice an alternative teaching method that they have not already seen. Answer b is incorrect because flash cards tend to be difficult for students who struggle with math because they are unable to memorize facts easily. Answer d is incorrect because although group projects may be beneficial to some students, their use may not support students who struggle with memorizing facts.

19. C: Although all of these choices can be effective in helping a student achieve their ultimate goal, the postsecondary transition goal is simply what the student is seeking to achieve. Although the goal does have to be realistic and something that the student is interested in, the goal may or may not be met in the future. Postsecondary transition goals in the area of employment are important in guiding the students toward careers that they may have an interest in pursuing. Answer a is incorrect because going to college is an example of an education goal. Answer b is incorrect because researching the job requirements is more of listing the steps the student will take to reach the goal. Answer d is incorrect because this is more about what will help him reach his ultimate goal.

20. D: Although all of these factors can have an enormous impact on a person and everyone may be impacted in a different way, the support system is typically the most beneficial. Without a support system in place, which may include parents, siblings, or other friends or family members, it will be difficult for individuals with disabilities to follow their own path to making a positive impact on society. Research shows that individuals with disabilities are more likely to succeed when they have a positive support system. Answer a is incorrect because although the type of disability is certainly impactful, individuals with all kinds of disabilities can succeed with proper support. Answer b is incorrect because the personality is important, but it does not have as much of an impact as a support system in place. Answer c is incorrect because the meaning of the disability may or may not be impactful for some individuals.

21. D: The purpose of the prereferral process is to put supports in place before obtaining consent for a special education evaluation. Obtaining consent would typically occur after the referral for special education services rather than during the prereferral process. The prereferral process is important in determining whether or not the student needs to be evaluated for special education services. Answer a is incorrect because evaluating a student's strengths and weaknesses is important to determine which supports need to be put into place. Answer b is incorrect because putting accommodations and interventions into place is helpful in evaluating what works for a student and what doesn't. Answer c is incorrect because evaluating the accommodations and interventions is important in deciding if they need to be continued or if another action should take place.

22. A: Although it is typically thought of as a good teaching practice to incorporate different kinds of activities in a lesson, some students struggle with this change. Students with autism or ADHD may have a harder time adjusting to their daily routine being adjusted. Incorporating some elements of the same activity every day might be best for some students' needs. Answer b is incorrect because even if students do not all have the knowledge that is required, the activity might be designed to give them that knowledge. Answer c is incorrect because it is best practice to monitor which students can work together and which students cannot. Answer d is incorrect because it is important to implement which activities a student can complete according to their IEP, but each student should still feel included in the class.

23. D: Although it is possible that all of these choices can be beneficial in certain circumstances, an 11th-grade student tutoring a 9th grader is the most appropriate. It is important for the students to be close in age to be considered peers and for the tutor to be mature. For students with disabilities who are being tutored, it is also best if the student who is tutoring is the same age or older to avoid having a student who is lacking confidence. Answer a is incorrect because a student in 2nd grade may or may not be mature enough to tutor another student. Answer b is incorrect because the peer tutor model tends to work better when the students are closer in age. Answer c is incorrect because it is best to have the tutor be someone who is older or the same age as the student who needs the tutoring.

24. C: Preventive strategies typically include what will be done in order to free students from the items or events that typically cause these behaviors. These may include removing a student from distractions or allowing them to run around the gym if they need it. These strategies can be used to help alleviate some of the behaviors once the triggers are determined. Answer a is incorrect because identifying the behaviors typically belongs in the "description of behavior" section of the plan. Answer b is incorrect because behaviors that serve a similar purpose as the unwanted behavior are called replacement behaviors. Answer d is incorrect because teaching the individual skills is considered the teaching strategies.

25. C: The service delivery section of the IEP describes what services a student will be provided and the nature of those services. This may include the amount of time that a student receives these services for and who will provide the services. This section is crucial in describing the services that must be provided and ensuring that the services are provided for an allotted amount of time. Answer a is incorrect because the present levels section describes how a student is currently performing. Answer b is incorrect because the accommodations section of the IEP describes the accommodations that the student will be provided in the general education setting. Answer d is incorrect because the prior written notice section of the IEP describes the changes that were discussed at the IEP meeting.

26. A: Although functional curriculum can be implemented for students of any age or disability, it is most often taught to students with intellectual disabilities. Functional curriculum focuses on life skills and other daily living skills that students will need after high school. It may be appropriate for certain students to start working on some of these skills as early as the elementary school level. Answer b is incorrect because students with specific learning disabilities likely would not access this curriculum until high school. Answer b is incorrect because students with speech or language impairments are not likely to need this curriculum to supplement their knowledge. Answer d is incorrect because students with developmental delays may or may not access this curriculum later on, but the elementary school age tends to be early for most students.

27. D: Although there may be many benefits to holding an externally facilitated IEP meeting, it typically takes a little longer for the special education teacher to prepare. The purpose of the externally facilitated IEP meeting is to include everyone in the conversation using an outside facilitator who may or may not know the student. The external facilitator will need to meet with the special education teacher beforehand in order to get an understanding of the student, which tends to take extra time. Answer a is incorrect because the facilitated IEP is designed to be focused and handle one issue at a time. Answer b is incorrect because part of the facilitator's role is to ensure that they can problem solve whenever a conflict does arise. Answer c is incorrect because everyone on the IEP team will be included in the discussion at a facilitated IEP meeting.

28. A: Although reaching out to colleges in the area may or may not result in responses from those schools, they are most likely to respond if they hear from Gordon. It is important for Gordon to feel empowered to reach out to these schools on his own in order to develop independence. Involving Gordon in the process allows him to feel like he owns the experience and is making his own path for the future. Answer b is incorrect because assisting Gordon in researching colleges can help him narrow his choices. Answer c is incorrect because helping him find jobs he may want will allow him to find out what schools offer certain programs. Answer d is incorrect because allowing him to practice application writing will help him with the actual application procedure.

29. B: For students who have been evaluated for special education services and identified as not having a disability, it is important that they return to the general education setting with the supports that they were previously receiving. It is important to keep these supports in place because the student was determined ineligible. It is likely that these students will continue to need these accommodations to access the general education curriculum. Answer a is incorrect because removing the accommodations would likely result in the student struggling like they did before the special education referral. Answer c is incorrect because although a 504 referral may be appropriate for some students, this determination would likely come from the 504 team. Answer d is incorrect because it is best to refer students to supports that can be put in place in the school setting.

30. A: In order to attain a measurable goal, there must be concrete evidence that the goal is or is not being met. Without this evidence, it is difficult to determine how much progress is being made in the goal and how much is left to accomplish. Goals that are measurable are crucial to refining exactly what it is that the goal is trying to achieve. Answer b is incorrect because a cost analysis is a component of an attainable goal. Answer c is incorrect because a clarified description may be beneficial for whether or not a goal is measurable but is more closely related to the specificity of the goal. Answer d is incorrect because overarching objectives are components of relevant goals.

31. C: Although it may be a good idea to send home a note for some students, many times a note will get lost in the transition from school to home. It is important to make a good first impression, and it is not the best idea to take a chance on the note not making it to the parents. The first meeting or introduction as case manager is important due to the nature of the relationship that will occur with the student. Answer a is incorrect because calling them with an introduction is a great way to establish a connection with the parents. Answer b is incorrect because setting up a meeting, if done in a positive manner, can allow the parents and the teacher to get on the same page at the start. Answer d is incorrect because meeting them in person can always be an effective way to first get to know someone.

32. A: One of the challenges of identifying students who receive English learner services for special education is deciding whether or not their needs are related to a disability. It can be difficult to distinguish between a student with a disability and a student who is new to the language. It is crucial to take all of the steps that are necessary to ensure the correct placement of these students. Answer b is incorrect because if it is determined that a student is eligible for special education services, the IEP must meet their needs. Answer c is incorrect because special education services would be beneficial in providing the student access to the general education curriculum. Answer d is incorrect because the decision is based on whether or not services are needed for special education rather than the services they already received.

33. D: Although some children may want to start being more like their friends at Josh's age, this is an aspect of social development that typically comes later. This is a behavior that would likely occur after a child has spent more time with friends in order to learn more about them. This typically happens as children make friends and spend the majority of their time with them. Answer a is incorrect because showing some separation anxiety is typical of a student in preschool. Answer b is incorrect because cooperating with other children is expected from a child of this age. Answer c is incorrect because exploring independently is also to be expected.

34. A: Cooperative learning can be beneficial to students with all kinds of disabilities because it allows for smaller groups to work together. Rather than the teacher doing the majority of instructing, cooperative learning allows the students to work together to solve problems. Many students with disabilities may struggle to participate in large class discussions, but this gives them a different kind of opportunity to learn. Answer b is incorrect because there is likely going to be the same level of support in these classes. Answer c is incorrect because students tend to receive less direct instruction from teachers in cooperative learning classrooms. Answer d is incorrect because students may or may not make more progress on IEP goals depending on the student and the goals.

35. C: Although inquiry-based instruction can be beneficial for many students when learning math, many students that struggle will likely need more instruction and steps on how to solve problems. Inquiry-based instruction relies on the students to ask the questions, which can be difficult for struggling students. Students who struggle with math problem solving often struggle with vocabulary and executive functioning. Answer a is incorrect because explicit instruction can be beneficial so that students know exactly how to solve the problems. Answer b is incorrect because vocabulary development is beneficial to students who struggle with math problem solving and do not understand certain terminology. Answer d is incorrect because graphic organizers can help provide organizational support to students in solving math problems.

36. D: Although all of these choices can be beneficial in helping these students with tasks they may need after high school, having knowledge of grocery words will likely help them the most. These students are likely to visit grocery stores frequently and will need to be able to read certain words in order to make purchases. Functional curriculum can help students with skills they will need when they are finished with school. Answer a is incorrect because although reading street signs can help these students, they may or may not experience driving. Answer b is incorrect because reading textbooks will likely not be a skill they will need. Answer c is incorrect because even though these students will likely use computers throughout their life, this is something that can be self-taught or practiced at home.

37. C: Although all of these choices may be beneficial in helping understand the student, it is important to first understand why these behaviors occur. Asking a teacher to fill out a survey to discuss what is happening in class is the best way to determine how to better assess the student. The environment in which the behavior occurs is the best way to diagnose the behavior and in turn adapt or change the instructional strategies in place. Answer a is incorrect because having the students fill out a survey of preferences will likely not change their behavior in class. Answer b is incorrect because having parents answer a survey might not be beneficial because what happens at home is often different from what happens at school. Answer d is incorrect because simply having a list of potential behaviors is likely not enough to guide instruction.

38. A: The purpose of an intelligence test is to measure a student's ability to reason and solve problems, which includes thinking abstractly. Intelligence tests can provide valuable information in deciphering the reasons that a student may struggle in particular areas. These tests can be beneficial for students of all grades and disabilities for gathering information. Answer b is incorrect because measuring a student's spoken language abilities would be considered a processing assessment. Answer c is incorrect because measuring a student's ability to convey ideas through oral language would be considered a communication assessment. Answer d is incorrect because visual information assessments would typically fall under the visual-spatial assessment categories.

39. C: Although it may be beneficial to allow her to pass when she is called on in front of the class, this may also cause her to be self-conscious. She might not be comfortable speaking in front of the class, but she also may not want to pass. It is important to have a conversation with students like Alison to determine what they are comfortable with and how they can be best supported. Answer a is incorrect because allowing her to skip these oral presentations might make her feel less stress about talking in front of the class. Answer b is incorrect because giving her the opportunity to collaborate with peers that she knows can help her be supported in the class. Answer d is incorrect because allowing her to sit in front of the class might make it easier to access the teacher.

40. D: Practicing doing laundry every once in a while and in a separate location from where the skill was learned provides maintenance and generalization. This allows the student an opportunity to remember how to practice the skill but also complete it across various settings. Maintenance and generalization are important instructional strategies in providing opportunities for students to practice skills. Answer a is incorrect because practicing the skill every day in the same location does not provide maintenance or generalization. Answer b is incorrect because practicing the skill in the same location it was learned does not provide generalization. Answer c is incorrect because practicing the skill every day does not provide for the best maintenance when the student is first learning the skill rather than maintaining it.

41. D: For a student who is new to a classroom, it is important that the general education teacher and special education teacher come up with a plan together. This collaboration is crucial to the success of the student because preparation can limit potential issues that may arise. Although some students may not require as much preparation, students like Justin with deaf-blindness will likely require a plan in order to meet their needs. Answer a is incorrect because simply giving the teacher the IEP will likely not prepare them as much as a collaborative conversation. Answer b is incorrect because allowing the general education teacher to teach on their own without collaboration may leave them unprepared. Answer c is incorrect because although asking the district for assistance can be beneficial, working with the general education teacher will likely have a greater impact.

42. A: Part of the No Child Left Behind Act of 2001 stated that students with disabilities would be assessed just the same as their general education peers. One of the reasons for this was for schools to be held accountable for each and every student. This allowed the schools to determine whether or not new or different programs needed to be established in order to meet the needs of students with disabilities. Answer b is incorrect because the act did not state that schools needed to provide extra assistance to these students. Answer c is incorrect because IEPs were already established before this act was passed. Answer d is incorrect because schools were not required to provide these postsecondary opportunities.

43. A: Although all of these choices may have an impact in one way or another, being able to maintain a budget may be the most difficult. Even though a calculator may be used to maintain a budget, there are still many calculations involved. This is something that Mike is going to have to do for the rest of his life. Answer b is incorrect because although this may certainly impact Mike, he will likely not be using measurements as much as using his budget. Answer c is incorrect because the cashier at the store will typically calculate the correct change. Answer d is incorrect because although making a schedule can certainly impact a person with a math disability, there are many ways to overcome this such as using a calendar.

44. D: Students with executive functioning deficits often struggle to organize their thoughts or stay on task. Providing them with daily objectives allows them the opportunity to understand what is expected of them and to remain on task. It is important to continually review the objectives throughout the lesson so that students are reminded of what is expected. Answer a is incorrect because planning can be a difficult skill for students with executive functioning deficits. Answer b is incorrect because objectives typically are not designed as an assessment method. Answer c is incorrect because giving the student a task while they are learning is often difficult for those with executive functioning deficits.

45. B: The standard score in an assessment is used to give the student a numbered score in order to compare that number to the average. Many tests will consider 100 to be the average standard score based on the results of the assessments. Students will then be given standard scores that are compared to that average score. Answer a is incorrect because the standard deviation typically determines how spread out the numbers are. Answer c is incorrect because comparing the rank of the score to other students is considered the percentile rank. Answer d is incorrect because the hypothetical range of scores is considered the confidence interval.

46. C: Although all of these choices can be valuable in enhancing the learning experience for students in the class, creating experiences that they will enjoy and remember will likely have the greatest impact on the majority of students. A meaningful learning experience will likely include topics that the students enjoy and topics that they will remember. Students with disabilities will especially be more likely to take meaning from topics that they are interested in. Answer a is incorrect because although offering to help can certainly benefit the students, they may or may not find this meaningful to them. Answer b is incorrect because although getting to know each student can help them feel safe and secure in the class, this may not impact the meaning of the class. Answer d is incorrect because giving rewards to students may not have as much of a long-term impact on the students.

47. A: The present levels of academic achievement determine the current academic and social functioning in the academic environment. The present levels are crucial in establishing the foundation for the rest of the IEP based on how the student is currently functioning. This may include progress on goals, strengths, needs, and how the student is performing with regard to grades and other scores. Answer b is incorrect because the accommodations are typically determined in the accommodations section of the IEP. Answer c is incorrect because the disability category is determined before the IEP is written. Answer d is incorrect because the present levels section does not compare a student to peers and instead states how the student is currently performing.

48. D: Curriculum-based assessments can be beneficial in determining how much progress a student is making on their goals. It is important to monitor the progress a student is making by giving them curriculum-based assessments that are directed toward their IEP goals. These data can help to guide instruction and determine if any changes need to be made so that the student makes continued progress toward that goal. Answer a is incorrect because comparing a student's score to others in the district would be a norm-referenced or standardized assessment. Answer b is incorrect because comparing a student's score to their grade in the class would likely be a formative assessment. Answer c is incorrect because comparing a student's score to the average score would likely be a norm-referenced assessment.

49. C: The demonstration of learning should show whether or not a student met the daily objective. For students working on reading fluency, reading a short passage that is timed will show if they met the daily reading fluency objective. This is designed to be a quick assessment without any assistance from the teacher. Answer a is incorrect because reading a short story and answering questions may not be the best way to assess reading fluency. Answer b is incorrect because listening to a passage does not allow Brady to demonstrate his reading fluency ability. Answer d is incorrect because the demonstration of learning is designed to be an individual activity without assistance.

50. B: A diagnostic assessment can be valuable in determining what a student knows or is capable of learning. For students who may be new to a school or a class, it can be helpful to give them a diagnostic assessment to see where they might fit in best. It may be important to assess a student like Peyton before they are inappropriately placed in a class that may be too easy or too difficult for them. Answer a is incorrect because accessing accommodations would be more of a conversation at an IEP meeting rather than in the diagnostic assessment. Answer c is incorrect because assessing goals is likely something that occurs when discussing his IEP. Answer d is incorrect because modifications are likely not going to be added to a student's instruction based on the results of a diagnostic assessment.

51. A: In order to assess a student for oral expression abilities, a test to measure their expressive language abilities is most appropriate. Students who struggle with oral expression tend to struggle expressing themselves orally due to many factors. This kind of assessment can guide the data collection needed for instruction in the classroom and skills to work on. Answer b is incorrect because receptive language assessments are more appropriate for students who struggle with language input rather than output. Answer c is incorrect because auditory discrimination tests are used for students who struggle with different sounds. Answer d is incorrect because this kind of assessment would be more appropriate in measuring a student's cognitive abilities.

52. B: Audiobooks can be beneficial to students who struggle with reading comprehension. This is a good opportunity for someone like Jessica to take in the content without having to struggle with the reading. Using this technology can be beneficial to students who are still learning to read. Answer a is incorrect because simply researching her topic may not help her with reading. Answer c is incorrect because although giving a presentation may be beneficial, it is still important for her to read the content. Answer d is incorrect because allowing her to use her phone may be too distracting.

53. C: Although it could be beneficial to conduct a verbal intelligence test on all of these students, it would be most appropriate for a student with a writing disability. Students who struggle with communication, including writing, often struggle to express themselves. The verbal intelligence test measures this in order to determine if there are supports that can be put in place for students with these deficits. Answer a is incorrect because students with intellectual disabilities would likely struggle with these kinds of assessments. Answer b is incorrect because although students with math deficiencies may struggle with verbal intelligence, students who struggle with reading and writing are more likely to benefit from these tests. Answer d is incorrect because students with visual impairments will likely have a separate kind of assessment to measure their abilities in this area.

54. C: According to the IDEA definition of the least restrictive environment, students with disabilities must attend general education to the maximum extent possible. Although the least restrictive environment may be different for each student, it is important to consider the benefits of a student attending general education classes. Some students may access general education the majority of their day, whereas others may have limited access due to the impact of their disability. Answer a is incorrect because the least restrictive environment does not stipulate that students with IEPs must receive services. Answer b is incorrect because students with disabilities may or may not receive special education services. Answer d is incorrect because the least restrictive environment principle does not stipulate that students receive services in a separate environment.

55. B: Students with intellectual disabilities will oftentimes learn best by practicing the concepts rather than simply listening about them. It is beneficial for these students to do more hands-on activities as opposed to listening to lectures. The practical application gives them an opportunity to apply what they know. Answer a is incorrect because although background knowledge can be helpful, it does not give them the chance to show what they know. Answer c is incorrect because an assessment for students with intellectual disabilities may not be practical. Answer d is incorrect because independent practice might benefit some students with intellectual disabilities, but typically having more hands-on activities with others allows them to practice what they have learned.

56. A: The other health impairment category tends to identify the majority of students due to a diagnosis of attention-deficit/hyperactivity disorder (ADHD). Although boys may be identified for services more than girls in the majority of categories, it is overwhelmingly more so in the other health impairment category. According to the Centers for Disease Control and Prevention, boys are three times more likely to have ADHD than girls. Answer b is incorrect because the number of boys and girls with a specific learning disability tends to be fairly even. Answer c is incorrect because intellectual disabilities also do not have as large of a disparity as the other health impairment category. Answer d is incorrect because there is no correlation between gender and deaf-blindness.

57. D: Although computer-driven instruction is designed for students to be independent in completing their classes, it is important that the teacher checks in with the student to ensure progress. Students who complete classes online will likely need less support than other students, so it is important to give them that freedom. It is also important, however, to make sure that they know what they are doing and that they have someone who cares about their progress. Answer a is incorrect because reading the prompts to him likely will likely prove to be ineffective for this kind of student. Answer b is incorrect because although it may be beneficial to tutor him, it would likely be more productive to help him during school hours. Answer c is incorrect because just reviewing his grade does not necessarily show that he is being helped or supported.

58. C: Students with learning disabilities will likely use budgeting when they enter adulthood and continue to use it throughout their entire life. This is an example of a skill that can be incorporated into a lesson plan for all students, including those with disabilities. It is crucial to teach students with disabilities skills that are appropriate for them and can be used throughout their lifetime. Answer a is incorrect because students with Down syndrome will most likely not deal with the stock market. Answer b is incorrect because being able to read a newspaper may or may not be a skill that students with ADHD use throughout their life. Answer d is incorrect because creative writing may benefit some students with autism, but it is not likely to be a lifelong skill for everyone.

59. B: Although all of these choices could be potential conflicts in the co-teaching model, disagreeing on strategies is likely the greatest disadvantage. When teachers collaborate to teach a class, the general education teacher and special education teacher may have different approaches to certain topics and tasks. This may lead to some conflicts about the instructional strategies or how some of the students learn best. Answer a is incorrect because typically co-teaching will involve one teacher teaching more than the other. Answer c is incorrect because it is best to collaborate in subjects that teachers are familiar with in order to provide students with the best possible instruction. Answer d is incorrect because even if one teacher does not have as much experience, it is still possible to collaborate and learn from one another.

60. D: Although students with autism spectrum disorder may suffer from orthopedic impairments at a higher rate than their peers, this is not typically one of the co-occurring conditions. Students with autism tend to suffer from many mental and physical conditions. According to Autism Speaks, the largest autism advocacy organization in the United States, many of these conditions co-occur with students diagnosed with autism. Answer a is incorrect because anxiety is common with students with autism. Answer b is incorrect because epilepsy is also a commonly co-occurring condition with autistic students. Answer c is incorrect because sleep conditions are also very common.

61. C: Students with independent living skills goals will likely need some support in reaching their goals and will need to take it step by step. Researching ingredients that a student will need is a great first step in knowing what is needed to make the meals. It is important that students are supported in their independent living skills goals while also being given a level of independence. Answer a is incorrect because just working in the cafeteria and cleaning likely will not prepare the student to cook a meal. Answer b is incorrect because shadowing at a restaurant may be fun for the student, but hands-on experiences are likely to be more beneficial. Answer d is incorrect because if students are making lunch each day, they likely do not need this goal.

62. B: In situations in which students run out of the classroom, it is always important to ask for assistance. This way, someone can look out for the student to make sure that they are safe while also protecting the other students in the school. It is important that the safety of everyone in the school is ensured when a situation such as this arises. Answer a is incorrect because running after him could leave the classroom without supervision. Answer c is incorrect because calling the police may not be as beneficial as calling the office because they can help right away. Answer d is incorrect because although it will be important to call his parents later on, it is more important to seek help right away.

63. A: In order for students to learn from the lecture, it is important that they are able to practice it on their own. Students with significant needs may have a difficult time going straight from a lecture to independent practice, so guided practice is crucial. This gives them an opportunity to understand how to complete the practice. Answer b is incorrect because collaborative practice may not be as beneficial for students who need support from the teacher. Answer c is incorrect because independent practice for students with severe needs is a difficult task. Answer d is incorrect because student-led practice may not provide the results wanted without supervision from a teacher.

64. B: Although all of these choices could potentially be beneficial to a student like Jake, opportunities that allow him to gain experience with tasks will likely be the most helpful. Students with intellectual disabilities often struggle with abstract reasoning and tend to do better with more hands-on learning. Having someone come in to provide workshops will likely help Jake learn about independent living more than simply being offered information. Answer a is incorrect because although having someone from vocational rehabilitation come talk to him would be a great start, it might be better for him to have some kind of personal experience. Answer c is incorrect because having someone help him with recreational activities likely will not be as helpful as someone helping him with other skills. Answer d is incorrect because just giving a student like Jake flyers may not prove to be helpful.

65. C: Although parents have many rights with regard to their child's IEP, running the IEP is not one of those rights. Typically, the IEP meeting will be run by a special education teacher or administrator. Parents are encouraged to be highly involved in the IEP meeting, but they are not responsible for facilitating the meeting. Answer a is incorrect because parents are important members of the IEP team. Answer b is incorrect because parents can call an IEP meeting if they believe their child's needs must be addressed. Answer d is incorrect because parents can help to develop IEP goals.

66. D: The school nurse may have many roles and responsibilities, but one of them is to provide a health update for each eligibility meeting. It is important that the student's health concerns are updated to determine what impact they might have on a student's access to education. The school nurse may have more involvement for certain students on IEPs than others but is typically involved with each one at some point. Answer a is incorrect because the special education teacher typically serves as the case manager. Answer b is incorrect because the special education teacher also ensures that accommodations are put into place. Answer c is incorrect because the school counselor or social worker will likely implement mental health services.

67. C: Students who score in the below-average range on achievement tests with no other concerns will typically fall under the "specific learning disability" category. Students with specific learning disabilities have deficits in the areas of reading, writing, and math. It is important to understand the results of assessments in order to appropriately place students and provide services that the student will need. Answer a is incorrect because students with trouble in speech or communication would take a test specific to those needs. Answer b is incorrect because students who receive services under the other health impairment category will have a health impairment that impacts their access to education. Answer d is incorrect because a cognitive disability is not one of the disability categories under IDEA.

68. A: Although the results of standardized assessments can be valuable tools, it is difficult to monitor the progress of the students when these tests are taken infrequently. It is best to monitor student growth frequently in order to determine if new interventions need to be put in place. When relying on tests that are only taken once or twice per year, it can be difficult to monitor progress. Answer b is incorrect because curriculum-based assessments can be given to students at any time to chart their progress. Answer c is incorrect because classroom observations can be beneficial for evaluating students with behavior goals. Answer d is incorrect because classroom grades can help to determine which subjects a student may struggle with.

69. C: The Americans with Disabilities Act provides equal opportunities for those individuals with disabilities who seek employment or other services. These individuals cannot be discriminated against simply because they have a disability. Students who receive special education services should know these rights when accessing a job or other accommodations in the community. Answer a is incorrect because the provision of accommodations in the classroom comes from Section 504 of the Rehabilitation Act. Answer b is incorrect because FAPE is a right that comes from IDEA. Answer d is incorrect because the highly qualified teacher provision comes from the No Child Left Behind Act.

70. A: When assessing a student for fine motor skills, it is important to take a look at activities such as drawing, writing, and using scissors. These kinds of skills are considered fine movements in that they are smaller movements that involve the hands, wrists, fingers, or toes. These kinds of assessments are important for determining whether or not a student needs additional support with a skill such as handwriting. Answer b is incorrect because watching a student making numbers with their hands is more of a tactile assessment. Answer c is incorrect because watching a student throw a ball would be looking at gross motor abilities. Answer d is incorrect because watching a student riding a bike would also be looking at his gross motor skills.

71. B: Although all of these factors can have a significant impact on a student, the content the student has learned has the greatest impact on the special education identification process. Students may come from many different cultures and have learned different topics and ideas. The special education identification process will look at a student's progress and how much they know about certain subjects compared with their peers. Answer a is incorrect because although the language a student speaks is important, it does not necessarily correspond to whether or not they should receive special education services. Answer c is incorrect because knowing where a student comes from can be helpful, but it does not impact identification. Answer d is incorrect because religion also does not impact identification.

72. D: Although teaching a student with anxiety about stress-reducing activities can be beneficial, it may not be ideal to do it at the beginning of the class period. This could potentially make the student feel overwhelmed or that they have one more thing to deal with. Students with anxiety may thrive in a structured environment, but it is important to be judicial about the strategies used. Answer a is incorrect because having a pass to leave the class can allow the student to feel comfortable knowing that they have a release. Answer b is incorrect because many students have anxiety around tests, and it can be helpful for them to take their test in a quiet environment. Answer c is incorrect because breaking down assignments into pieces can make them seem more manageable and cause less stress.

73. C: Although some parents are difficult to contact and do not wish to be involved with their child's education, providing alternatives might be the best option. It is important to accommodate the needs of the parents whenever possible in an attempt to get them more involved. The input of the parents is very valuable at IEP meetings, so if having them participate by phone is the best option for them, then that should be explored. Answer a is incorrect because they are unlikely to respond if they continue to receive phone calls nonstop. Answer b is incorrect because although sending forms home may work for some parents, some kind of verbal communication would likely be more productive. Answer d is incorrect because it is important to have input from the family members that live with the student.

74. B: Although all of these objectives may be beneficial, they cannot necessarily be measured. The number of outbursts a student has over a given time period is something that can be calculated and measured. Measurable objectives should also be realistic for a student to achieve over a certain time period. Answer a is incorrect because it is impossible to measure how much a student's behavior improves without quantifiable data. Answer c is incorrect because it is difficult to measure social interactions. Answer d is incorrect because although it is possible to measure how much work a student completes, an objective must be more specific.

75. D: Diagnostic assessments are used to determine what students already know in order to develop the curriculum to be used. These kinds of tests include anything that is going to assess what the student's previous knowledge is before getting into the new content. This can be beneficial for students in special education in order to determine what interventions or supports they may need. Answer a is incorrect because pretests are a diagnostic that can be used to drive instruction. Answer b is incorrect because self-assessments can help the teacher understand what the student thinks of themselves. Answer c is incorrect because interviews can also be beneficial in understanding the needs of a student before designing the curriculum.

76. C: Students who receive services in the multiple disabilities category cannot be eligible in just one disability category. These students have more than one disability that impacts them to the point that one category does not meet their needs. According to IDEA, the combination of disabilities makes it so severe that they cannot be accommodated in one category. Answer a is incorrect because deaf-blindness has its own disability category. Answer b is incorrect because a student with an orthopedic impairment can be eligible for the multiple disabilities category if they are impacted by another disability as well. Answer d is incorrect because the impact of disabilities may change, and students can go from being identified as a student with multiple disabilities to a single disability over time.

77. D: It is likely not going to be useful to change curriculum for the next unit because of the performance of students. It will be more beneficial to take a look at some of the instructional strategies used and if there were ways to make the learning more meaningful and productive for the students being tested. This is especially the case for students with disabilities and meeting the needs of each student in the class. Answer a is incorrect because determining which kinds of questions that students struggled with can allow the teacher to redesign or modify those questions for the next test. Answer b is incorrect because identifying which students struggled allows the teacher to keep a closer eye on or accommodate some of these students. Answer c is incorrect because understanding the kinds of questions that the students asked can help to fill some of the holes that might have been left throughout the teaching.

78. A: Students who are at risk may find that classes that are closely related to the career they want to pursue are likely to be more meaningful. At-risk students tend to be bored or tired of the curriculum of the schools they attend and might be ready for a change. When students show signs of disinterest in certain topics but are passionate about their future, it is important to seek classes that they will enjoy and get meaning from. Answer b is incorrect because although students may find that they like the teachers and curriculum more, it is not likely due to the fact that the teachers are better. Answer c is incorrect because these classes would likely be the same length as the regular classes. Answer d is incorrect because although these students may find that the classes build community, this is not likely to be a reason to take the classes.

79. C: In order for students to maintain a skill, they will likely need to work on it periodically in order to remember it. Students likely do not need to work on it every day in order to maintain the skill — just once in a while. It is important for students to maintain their knowledge in order to continue building off it. Answer a is incorrect because a daily quiz is likely too much just to maintain the concept. Answer b is incorrect because just giving the students a study guide does not mean that they will practice the skill on their own. Answer d is incorrect because a test at the end of the unit does not allow them an opportunity to maintain the skill.

80. D: Assigning a mock interview is the most appropriate demonstration of knowledge when working on interviewing for a job. Summative assessments evaluate what a student learns from a particular unit, and a mock interview is the best way to demonstrate this knowledge. It is important for the summative assessment to show whether or not the student has the skills needed or the knowledge that was supposed to be gained in that unit. Answer a is incorrect because assigning a paper would not likely be very beneficial to students who are practicing for job interviews. Answer b is incorrect because a multiple-choice test would not help students as much as practicing the skills that they will need. Answer c is incorrect because although a presentation may be helpful, a mock interview would be more productive in seeing what a student is capable of by the end of the unit.

81. B: Although there can be many benefits of standardized tests for students with disabilities, one of the most useful is in determining class placement. These results show what a student is capable of doing, typically in the areas of reading, writing, and math, and comparing them with their peers. This allows teachers to best determine which instruction they are capable of receiving and what they still need to improve upon. Answer a is incorrect because standardized tests would likely not be able to determine which accommodations a student needs to access. Answer c is incorrect because IEP goals and objectives typically come from classroom instruction or achievement test data. Answer d is incorrect because the least restrictive environment for a student is dependent on many factors, not simply a standardized assessment.

82. C: Students with ADHD due to attention deficits will often make remarks in the classroom simply to get the teacher's attention. It might be better to simply ignore those remarks in the hopes that they might be eliminated. Although this will not work for every student, it can be beneficial in ensuring that these students understand who the authority in the classroom is. Answer a is incorrect because allowing students to establish guidelines can help them feel welcome in the class. Answer b is incorrect because rewards can often help in management of some of the behavior in the class. Answer d is incorrect because a points system can help to give the students something to strive for.

83. A: Although standard scores may vary based on the assessment, scores that fall below 15 points of the standard score are considered below average. Because Hailey's score is less than 85, or 15 points less than the average score of 100, this would be considered below-average intelligence This information can be important in determining what a student is capable of and how to drive instruction for this kind of student because of the impact it may have. Answer b is incorrect because a score of 75 would be in the below-average rather than in the low-average range. Answer c is incorrect because mid average is not typically a range of a score when interpreting these results. Answer d is incorrect because assessments typically do not have a category that is labeled well below average.

84. C: One of the most important roles of the special education teacher is to ensure that the teachers of students with IEPs have access to their accommodations. It is important that teachers understand what they need to do in order to support students with disabilities in the classroom. Without knowing these accommodations, students may not receive the instruction that must be provided according to their IEP. Answer a is incorrect because ensuring that a student is on track to graduate is the job of the school counselor. Answer b is incorrect because although the special education teacher can assist in finding school supplies for a student, it is typically not their responsibility. Answer d is incorrect because it is also not the special education teacher's job to keep the student's permanent file up to date.

85. D: When working with a student that is suspected to be a victim of abuse, it is not always beneficial to dig deep into what has occurred. Although some students may be open to sharing what has happened to them, others may not, and they might feel pressured. Many students with disabilities are victims of neglect and abuse and they have a higher likelihood than their peers of being victims. Answer a is incorrect because listening to the student to hear what they have to say will calm them and help discover information. Answer b is incorrect because reporting the incident to child services is mandatory. Answer c is incorrect because continuing to teach them will provide normalcy for the students rather than treating them differently.

86. B: A child that is between the ages of 2 and 6 will typically start to use perception in their thought process. Children at this age tend to be able to solve simple problems rather than complex, multidimensional ones. Psychologist Jean Piaget proposed that a child's intellectual development progresses through four stages. Answer a is incorrect because a child that is manipulating objects would typically be younger than 2. Answer c is incorrect because a child that applies logical reasoning will likely be older than 7. Answer d is incorrect because a child that has abstract thoughts will likely be 12 or older.

87. C: Although all of these choices might be beneficial to some students in improving behavior, observing her regularly can help evaluate her behavior. If a student like Lisa is evaluated regularly, the causes of her behavior can be analyzed in order to guide instruction. It is important to constantly be thinking of new instructional practices and methods to support students with behavior struggles like Lisa. Answer a is incorrect because asking her to participate in class discussions might bring out more of the negative behavior that she tends to exhibit. Answer b is incorrect because although conferring with her might be beneficial in the short term, it is likely that her defiance will continue to arise unless the instruction changes. Answer d is incorrect because this would not be considered an assessment method but rather an instructional practice.

88. C: The constructivist learning theory states that the learner is the constructor of knowledge. The knowledge that a person has acquired allows them to construct the meaning and interpretation of that meaning. Understanding how students learn can provide insight into how they can be taught efficiently. Answer a is incorrect because this is an example of the behaviorist learning theory. Answer b is incorrect because these thoughts being shaped by mental processes is an example of the cognitive learning theory. Answer d is incorrect because the growth of the whole person is an example of the humanist learning theory.

89. C: If a student like Pat has been receiving services enough to collect a sufficient amount of data, a special education referral is warranted. If Pat has not made much progress in his reading fluency for six weeks, it is possible that he has a disability. It is important to give the student enough time to access the interventions and see if any kind of progress is made before referring the student to special education. Answer a is incorrect because although the length of the intervention may vary for certain students, six weeks is typically sufficient. Answer b is incorrect because discontinuing interventions may be detrimental to Pat as he continues to struggle with reading fluency. Answer d is incorrect because referral to a 504 plan would likely not be warranted because special education may be more appropriate given Pat's needs.

90. B: Although all of these laws play a role in supporting students with disabilities, the Individuals with Disabilities Education Act (IDEA) governs special education services. IDEA is responsible for ensuring that students with disabilities are given their rights and supports that meet their needs. IDEA is instrumental and protecting not only students with disabilities but also teachers and other providers that work with students with disabilities. Answer a is incorrect because Section 504 is a civil rights act that protects everyone with disabilities, not just students. Answer c is incorrect because the Family and Educational Rights and Privacy Act protects students in the confidentiality in the protection of information related to that student. Answer d is incorrect because it is a civil rights act that gives the same rights to everyone regardless of disability.

91. B: A disability that significantly affects verbal communication and social interaction falls under the "autism spectrum disorder disability" category. An emotional disturbance is a condition with certain characteristics that occurs over a period of time and affects a child's educational performance. According to IDEA, students that display characteristics of autism will typically fall under the autism spectrum disorder category. Answer a is incorrect because students with emotional disturbances often have an inability to learn that cannot be explained by these factors. Answer c is incorrect because these students often have a difficult time building relationships. Answer d is incorrect because fears associated with school are also common for students with an emotional disturbance.

92. B: Students with math deficiencies at the kindergarten level will likely need instruction and practice on basic concepts. Before students can begin more complex skills such as adding and subtracting, they must be able to identify numbers. A learning objective that relates to identifying numbers would be considered most appropriate for students who are struggling with math. Answer a is incorrect because adding is likely a skill that they will not have learned yet. Answer c is incorrect because subtracting numbers is a difficult skill for kindergarten students. Answer d is incorrect because counting to 100 would likely be too difficult.

93. D: Although all of these choices can be instrumental in establishing a safe classroom, building and maintaining relationships is the best long-term strategy for maintaining a safe classroom environment. When students feel important and there is a sense of trust with the teacher, the students will feel safer. If students do not have someone they can rely on, they will have a difficult time feeling safe. Answer a is incorrect because simply showing students where the exits are might not make them feel safe all the time. Answer b is incorrect because having a clean and orderly classroom is important, but it may not mean as much if the students do not feel valued. Answer c is incorrect because having the rules posted on the wall does not build a connection with the student that might make them feel safe.

94. C: Although text-to-speech software can benefit most students, it is typically designed for students with reading disabilities such as dyslexia. The text is read to the students, which allows them to comprehend what they read without having to read the print. This kind of device allows students with disabilities such as dyslexia access the general education curriculum by reading the same texts as their general education peers. Answer a is incorrect because although students with autism can access this kind of device, it is more often for students who struggle with reading fluency. Answer b is incorrect because students with hearing impairments would struggle to hear the text being transcribed by the device. Answer d is incorrect because students with multiple disabilities would likely have an alternate curriculum or access modifications rather than having assistive technology devices.

95. D: Hesitating to contact a student's family because of the community that they live in is an example of a cultural bias. Being unfamiliar with a student's community should not necessarily be a reason to hesitate contacting the family. It is important to get to know students, but it is also important to understand that there are going to be some cultural differences between the student and teacher. Answer a is incorrect because simply having a negative encounter in the past does not necessarily mean that there is a cultural bias. Answer b is incorrect because not knowing the family history does not mean there is a bias; it simply means that the teacher is uninformed. Answer c is incorrect because an experience with the student's sibling does not necessarily indicate that there is a bias toward that culture.

96. D: Reading comprehension is a skill that a student in ninth grade will likely need to focus on and will be most beneficial going forward. Although students can still focus on other skills if they have deficits, reading comprehension is a skill that they will use in each of their classes. There are many accommodations and other strategies to put into place if students have yet to master the other components of reading. Answer a is incorrect because fluency is a skill that can be continually practiced but is no longer a focus for the majority of students at the high school level. Answer b is incorrect because students will struggle with vocabulary if they do not comprehend what they read.

Answer c is incorrect because phonics is a skill that younger readers focus on and not typically high school students.

97. B: There are a variety of types of emotional disturbances that can impact the way they learn and process both stressful and typical environments. The most generally appropriate strategy for helping Christina complete her work is to modify the environment by allowing her to work in a separate setting if she is unable to focus in the typical setting. Stress management techniques should also be taught, but they are a less-direct method of helping Christina achieve in her classwork. Rewards for completing work may be additionally helpful in strengthening Christina's ability to stay calm and focused under stress, but they are generally not helpful in reducing stress after it has already initiated. Rewards are a method of cognitive-behavioral therapy, which can be an effective method of teaching a student how to handle stressful situations or re-direct their own thinking patterns. Implemented incorrectly, behavior reinforcement can backfire and cause the negative behavior to be reinforced, rather than the intended behavior management skill. Providing Christina with choices about what work she does is not likely to be the best overall situation as she needs to complete the work that is required by the curriculum. If she is able to perform the work that is assigned with more minimal modification, that is the better option.

98. C: Although it is not always easy or possible to eliminate every bias that a person might have, it is important not to make any assumptions. It is important to be sensitive to student needs especially when working with students with disabilities or from various cultural backgrounds. Assessments should be geared toward the content that students should know rather than the opinions that a teacher may have. Answer a is incorrect because it may not always be possible or realistic to get to know the background of every student in the class. Answer b is incorrect because each assessment will be different, and it may not be possible or the best assessment of student knowledge to include multicultural questions. Answer d is incorrect because it is not appropriate or the best practice to evaluate each student differently.

99. C: Although all of these factors may influence each student in a different way, knowing the population of the school can have the greatest impact. Knowing the populace of the school, whether that be students, teachers, or others, can make students feel safe inside the building. Students with disabilities may struggle with adjusting to a new environment, but building positive relationships can often be beneficial. Answer a is incorrect because although the location of the school may be important to some, the people in the building tend to have more of an impact. Answer b is incorrect because the climate of the school typically does not have a positive or negative impact. Answer d is incorrect because the size of the school can be important to some students, but it is more often the population that is most important.

100. C: Setting goals for students in order to give them something to strive for and providing an opportunity for success can build self-esteem. Without this self-esteem, students will lack confidence and not be able to accomplish as much. According to Maslow's hierarchy of needs, human needs are arranged in a hierarchy and can provide value in seeking to motivate students. Answer a is incorrect because using fear is not a tactic that will allow students to find security. Answer b is incorrect because establishing structure, although it may be beneficial to some students, will likely not help those students find self-actualization unless creativity is allowed. Answer d is incorrect because proving food may not be the best long-term motivational strategy.

101. C: Although each one of these living scenarios is possible, the most likely scenario for Billy is that he lives with his parents. Students with intellectual disabilities typically do not have the independent living skills to live on their own, so they tend to remain with their parents. Although there are certainly other options such as residential facilities, research shows that living with parents tends to be the most popular. Answer a is incorrect because living alone is likely not going to be the most common. Answer b is incorrect because although living in an apartment with others is likely more beneficial than living alone, it is still uncommon. Answer d is incorrect because there tend to be more benefits to living with parents rather than in a residential facility, such as cost and access to services.

102. D: The cognitive learning theory states that learning occurs through a process in which people internalize their thoughts in order to provide information. Discussions are an example of how the internalization of information can be shared with others. Understanding the cognitive learning theory can help one understand how learning occurs. Answer a is incorrect because repetitive practice is an example of an application of the behaviorist learning theory. Answer b is incorrect because research projects are an example of the application of the constructivist learning theory. Answer c is incorrect because collaborative learning is also an example of the constructivist learning theory in which knowledge is constructed based on individual experiences.

103. C: When students pose a safety risk to themselves or other students, it is important that they are removed from the classroom. Because of this, they may not always have access to the general education curriculum. Although it is always best practice to provide students access to the general education curriculum to the maximum extent possible, there are certainly exceptions such as this. Answer a is incorrect because students that need reading support should still access the general education class with additional support. Answer b is incorrect because modifications can be applied in the general education setting. Answer d is incorrect because behavior plans can also be implemented in the general education environment.

104. B: Although all of these environments may provide positive opportunities for the students, being in a smaller environment that is more intimate can be beneficial in getting to know the students. It is also helpful to have students with difficulties in emotional regulation sit at separate desks in case issues were to arise. It is important for the students to be in an environment that promotes safety and makes them feel valued. Answer a is incorrect because a large classroom wouldn't be as intimate and would likely make students uncomfortable. Answer c is incorrect because an office setting would likely cause students to be too close to each other, which may cause boundary issues among the students. Answer d is incorrect because having students sit at the same table may cause too much stimulation among peers.

105. A: Time samples are beneficial in recording observations in that they provide the frequency of a behavior. Teachers can tally how often a specific behavior occurred or how long an incident lasted. This can help teachers determine the appropriate next steps in order to target the behavior and reduce its frequency. Answer b is incorrect because observation checklists typically help to identify what the behaviors are. Answer c is incorrect because narratives are designed to give a summary of what a student or a group of students did. Answer d is incorrect because anecdotal records recall brief incidents that occur in order to give a picture of a specific event that happened.

106. B: When teaching students with coexisting disabilities, it is important to look at the student as a whole rather than someone with more than one disability. It is difficult to meet each and every need of the student if they are looked at separately. It is important to look at the student as a whole and discover how their needs can be met. Answer a is incorrect because it may be difficult to separate the disabilities in the individual student. Answer c is incorrect because although it is important to teach to the most impacted disability, there may be other needs as well. Answer d is incorrect because it could be difficult to teach to multiple disabilities at once.

107. A: Although all of these choices can be beneficial to students with traumatic brain injuries, allowing them the use of a computer is most productive with regard to writing. The use of a computer can help alleviate some of the stress and anxiety associated with the written product. Students with traumatic brain injuries often struggle with stress and anxiety, and using a computer can help with this. Answer b is incorrect because providing review sheets would be beneficial after instruction but not likely during a writing lesson. Answer c is incorrect because reducing distractions may help with focus but not specifically with the writing process. Answer d is incorrect because although slowing the pace will help students catch up, it likely will not help them with their writing.

108. C: It is important to move throughout the classroom periodically to ensure that students are on track academically and behaviorally while also keeping the teacher engaged. If the teacher stays in one spot during the entire class, students are more likely to act out or become a safety concern. Answer a is incorrect because just standing at the front of the class makes it difficult to monitor the progress of each student. Answer b is incorrect because walking around the classroom the entire time can potentially cause distractions to certain students. Answer d is incorrect because sitting with the students may be personable but could become an issue in accessing students who need support or may become safety concerns.

109. C: Although the system can be great in implementing a consistent, school-wide approach, it is often based around rewards. This can potentially alienate students with behavior struggles because they will be less likely to receive these rewards. It is important with a system such as this to try and make it fair and achievable for each and every student. Answer a is incorrect because these systems are designed to be implemented school-wide. Answer b is incorrect because students with IEPs can be involved just as much as every other student. Answer d is incorrect because the system tends to focus more on positive behavior rather than punishments.

110. A: One of the health problems that is included in the other health impairment category, according to the Individuals with Disabilities Education Act (IDEA), is asthma. A student with an other health impairment has limited strength, vitality, or alertness due to an acute health problem. If a student has an acute case of asthma that impacts their ability to function in the educational environment, they may be eligible for the other health impairment category. Answer b is incorrect because cerebral palsy would fall into the "orthopedic impairment" category. Answer c is incorrect because traumatic brain injury has its own category. Answer d is incorrect because a student with a perceptual disability would fall under the "specific learning disability" category.

111. A: The occupational therapist is responsible for assisting students in improving their fine motor skills such as handwriting. Many occupational therapists assist these students in the school setting in improving skills such as writing and cutting paper. Students with traumatic brain injuries may need help recovering by receiving support from an occupational therapist. Answer b is incorrect because physical therapists tend to focus on gross motor skills such as walking and other movements rather than fine motor skills. Answer c is incorrect because although the school nurse can assist in communicating with the physical therapist, they would not provide these services. Answer d is incorrect because the physical education teacher would teach many of these skills but not provide professional services to improve them.

112. A: Behavior rating scales are designed for teachers or parents to fill out in order to determine specific behaviors. These are typically compared with the results of other students in order to determine which behavior a student may struggle with. These can help to determine which accommodations or services need to be put in place in order to support students. Answer b is incorrect because simply performing evaluations would be helpful but would not be a part of the behavior rating scale. Answer c is incorrect because asking teachers to interview Susan would not indicate which behaviors are being exhibited in the classroom setting. Answer d is incorrect because a written assessment likely would not assist in evaluating student behavior.

113. B: Although all of these choices may provide appropriate strategies to differentiate instruction in certain circumstances, grouping students by ability level may not always be appropriate. Differentiated instruction means using instructional strategies to meet the needs of all of the students in the class. If students are grouped by ability level, the lower skilled students in the class may lose confidence or struggle with the assignment that is given. Answer a is incorrect because designing multiple activities, although it may take more work, can be an effective strategy. Answer c is incorrect because formative assessments can also be a valuable form of differentiating instruction. Answer d is incorrect because although lowering the expectations may not work for every student, it can be an effective method to level the playing field for certain students.

114. D: Children around the age of 8 who are in third grade begin to have a hard time handling criticism. These students will often struggle with failure and how to handle the responses of others. According to a Northeast Foundation for Children study, handling criticism is typical of a third-grade student. Answer a is incorrect because having difficulty managing emotions is behavior that would be expected of a typical third grader. Answer b is incorrect because keeping boundaries is a skill that most third graders would have learned. Answer c is incorrect because keeping boundaries is also a behavior that a typical third grader would have.

115. C: Although each student may respond differently to challenging tasks, many students with ADHD will shut down if a task becomes too difficult. It is important to understand and recognize what the student is able to accomplish before challenging them. It can be embarrassing or cause anxiety for students who are unable to fulfill the challenge of the teacher. Answer a is incorrect because offering choices to the students allows them to feel like they are a part of the decision making. Answer b is incorrect because hands-on learning activities allow students to get up and move around. Answer d is incorrect because repeating the instructions often ensures that each student hears what is expected and does not forget.

116. A: In order for students to be able to generalize a skill or concept, it is important for them to practice it across various settings. Practicing name writing inside the same classroom where it was taught does not generalize this skill. It is also important to not only practice in different settings but also with assistance from a variety of people. Answer b is incorrect because practicing at home with their parents can be an effective way to generalize this skill. Answer c is incorrect because practicing in art class gives them a new environment in which to work on the same skills. Answer d is incorrect because practicing with friends can also be beneficial in generalizing the skill.

117. C: By the time a student is in kindergarten at the age of 5 or 6, it is expected that they will have the motor skills to be able to use scissors. This is a skill that typically develops around the age of 4. According to the CanChild Centre for Childhood Disability Research, the average child is able to cut a line across paper by the age of 4. Answer a is incorrect because typing on a keyboard is a skill that typically develops around the age of 7. Answer b is incorrect because shoe tying is a skill that develops around the age of 7. Answer d is incorrect because tying a knot is a skill that tends to develop at age 6.

118. A: A student with an academic delay would not be eligible for the "developmental delay" category, according to IDEA. The category includes many areas, but it does not specify academics as one of them. Instead, the criteria include cognitive development but do not use the term "academic development." Answer b is incorrect because a student with a social development delay would be eligible according to IDEA criteria. Answer c is incorrect because adaptive delays are also listed under the IDEA definition. Answer d is incorrect because a delay in physical development would also determine a child to be eligible as a student with a developmental delay.

119. A: The goal of a summative assessment is to evaluate what a student has learned over a specific topic or topics. Summative assessments are typically graded and may include some kind of a test or paper that the students are responsible for. Summative assessments can be valuable for students with disabilities for many reasons including assessing a student's progress on IEP goals or whether or not a student's supports have been beneficial. Answer b is incorrect because determining appropriate instruction would be considered a diagnostic assessment. Answer c is incorrect because monitoring student learning would be considered a formative assessment. Answer d is incorrect because comparing students to a norm would be considered a norm-referenced or standardized assessment.

120. B: It is important to have closure in a lesson so students have a firm grasp on the concepts they were expected to learn that particular day. Closure gives the students clarity if there was any confusion about what they were supposed to learn. Students with disabilities may need extra reminders, and closure can help with this. Answer a is incorrect because closure typically happens before or after the assessment as a method of recapping what was taught. Answer c is incorrect because the demonstration of knowledge is typically a task that the student completes so the teacher knows that they understood the task. Answer d is incorrect because although closure may connect to objectives that may be coming in the future, it mostly relates to the tasks completed within that day.

121. D: Although all of these choices can be beneficial for certain groups of students, establishing a contract may overwhelm the student and give them yet something else to do. Students who are at risk will likely struggle to complete their work and seem distant from their peers and teachers. It is important to reach out to these students as soon as possible to determine how they can be helped. Answer a is incorrect because a peer tutor can give them a friend or show them that they have someone that cares about them. Answer b is incorrect because lightening their load can make some of their tasks seem doable. Answer c is incorrect because talking to this student and getting to know them a little more may motivate them to want to work a little harder.

122. D: Although each student is different and may require a different level of support, it is best practice for students to work on and improve their behavior management in the general education setting. It is important to have support in place for students, but they are most likely to develop these skills in the setting in which they display them most often. If students are pulled from class right away, they might miss valuable instruction or opportunities to improve their behavior in that setting. Answer a is incorrect because it might be a good idea to see how students are able to adjust before working on these skills right away. Answer b is incorrect because it is likely more productive for students to work through their issues with support rather than being removed from class right away. Answer c is incorrect because students can receive these services at any time regardless of whether they have a behavior plan.

123. A: Multisensory techniques have proven to be beneficial when teaching students who struggle with reading fluency. Many students who struggle are kinesthetic or visual learners and do better when they can see or manipulate the letter. This kind of strategy focuses on breaking down the letters in the words rather than the whole-word approach. Answer b is incorrect because metacognitive strategies include thinking strategies that would be involved with comprehension. Answer c is incorrect because text structuring involves breaking down sentences rather than letters. Answer d is incorrect because explicit teaching tends to be more productive when working on reading comprehension.

124. B: For students with specific learning disabilities, achievement tests are beneficial in gathering information about where the student may be deficient. Achievement tests such as the Wechsler Individual Achievement Test correspond with the categories associated with specific learning disabilities. This information is valuable in assessment of where students need improvement and potential strategies for instruction. Answer a is incorrect because this kind of assessment would be more appropriate for a younger student who is new to school. Answer c is incorrect because this assessment is typically used for those students who are at least 16 years old. Answer d is incorrect because this kind of assessment is an intelligence test rather than an achievement test.

125. D: Extended school year services are provided to students who struggle to retain information over the course of long breaks such as the summer. Some students who are determined eligible for these services receive addition schooling, typically sometime in the summer. This allows the students to retain some of the skills that they may forget over the course of extended breaks. Answer a is incorrect because not all students are determined eligible for extended school year services. Answer b is incorrect because there is not a set time period in which the services must be provided. Answer c is incorrect because extended school year services are typically provided sometime in the summer and not necessarily before the school year starts.

126. B: Students in seventh grade with specific learning disabilities in the area of writing would be expected to be able to write a paragraph. Some students may have more skills than others, but most students would be able to write a paragraph. This objective may need to be modified for certain students with more severe struggles, but a student with a specific learning disability that is appropriately placed would be expected to keep up with the curriculum. Answer a is incorrect because writing sentences would likely be a skill that students would have already mastered by this age. Answer c is incorrect because being able to write an essay likely would not be expected of seventh-grade students. Answer d is incorrect because simply writing words is a skill that these students already know.

127. A: One of the disadvantages to teaching students individually is that they cannot interact with their peers. It can be beneficial for students to work with their peers in order to build social skills and learn from each other. Although there are many advantages to one-on-one groups, many students learn best with other students. Answer b is incorrect because students are not accessing the general education curriculum in pull-out groups whether they are individuals or small groups. Answer c is incorrect because students also don't have access to general education teachers in any kind of special education pull-out group. Answer d is incorrect because students have access to the special education curriculum with either pull-out group type.

128. C: Although all of these grouping patterns have their own strengths and weaknesses, it makes the least sense to group students based on their disability. It is important to take into consideration many aspects including disability, but this is unlikely to be the determining factor. It is more important that the students in the group are a good match for the instruction and each other than what their disability might be. Answer a is incorrect because grouping students by ability can be effective in ensuring that the students learn at a similar pace. Answer b is incorrect because grouping by age can help ensure the students are learning the same content in class. Answer d is incorrect because grouping students by behavior can help make sure that students work well with each other.

129. D: Although the resource room can be a valuable environment for special education teachers to teach in, it is considered a setting rather than a service delivery model. Service delivery models indicate how the students will receive instruction rather than where the instruction will take place. It is important to consider the needs of the students before determining which kind of service model will be implemented. Answer a is incorrect because co-teaching can be beneficial when working with a general education teacher. Answer b is incorrect because pull-out groups can help students build on the skills that they struggle with. Answer c is incorrect because pushing into classrooms can help to support students who need additional assistance with the curriculum.

130. B: Kayla's science teacher would be included as a member of the IEP team because they are a general education teacher. It is important to have the input of at least one general education teacher at an IEP meeting. Having a science teacher at the meeting would be appropriate because Kayla has a disability in the area of math and science is closely related to math. Answer a is incorrect because the school counselor is not required to attend IEP meetings and likely would not attend the meeting. Answer c is incorrect because the school psychologist typically would not be a member of the IEP team for a student with a specific learning disability unless they had administered some kind of testing for the student's evaluation. Answer d is incorrect because school social workers do not typically serve as members of IEP teams unless the student has mental health concerns.

131. A: Embodied learning allows students to participate in activities that get the whole body involved. It allows students to move while still learning the content. Many students struggle to sit and learn all day, so this kind of instruction allows them to get up and move. It is important to provide a variety of learning activities in order to meet the needs of all of the students in the class. Answer b is incorrect because inquiry-based learning involves having students ask questions in order to learn. Answer c is incorrect because blended learning involves a combination of online and traditional learning. Answer d is incorrect because service learning typically involves students going out into the community to learn.

132. D: In order to assess younger students who may be experiencing difficulties with development, a developmental assessment can be helpful. These assessments determine the areas of strength and weakness for students and what they need to improve upon. This allows the teacher to figure out what areas need to be focused on more and if any additional supports need to be put in place for Sally. Answer a is incorrect because IQ assessments tend to evaluate the cognitive abilities of older students. Answer b is incorrect because curriculum-based assessments are used to determine the progress a student is making on their IEP goals. Answer c is incorrect because alternate assessments are used for students who do not take the typical standardized assessments.

133. A: Students are eligible to receive support for each one of the disability categories that they are identified in. Because of this, Trevor can receive academic support as a student with a specific learning disability and emotional support as a student with an emotional disturbance. Although students do not necessarily need to be identified as having more than one eligibility category to receive these supports, the identification of each one of these makes the services mandatory. Answer b is incorrect because Trevor would not automatically be eligible for a self-contained classroom. Answer c is incorrect because Trevor can have a behavior plan without being identified with co-occurring conditions. Answer d is incorrect because alternative placement is not determined based on co-occurring conditions.

134. B: One of the best ways to provide access to a student with a disability in the area of reading comprehension is to provide accommodations. Reading the text to the student allows them to take in what they are reading and process it more clearly than they might if reading independently. Typically, it would not be as beneficial to modify or change the expectations of what the student completes. Answer a is incorrect because modifying what the student reads does not allow them to access the curriculum that their peers are accessing. Answer c is incorrect because modifying the assignment may not give the student a chance to learn all of the material. Answer d is incorrect because giving a student fewer questions does not give them access to all of the curriculum.

135. C: Although these are examples of assistive technology devices, the FM listening system is typically used for students to listen to the speech of someone else. Students like George who struggle with writing will likely benefit more from devices that can help with the writing process. Assistive technology can be beneficial in helping students to access the general education curriculum despite their disability. Answer a is incorrect because graphic organizers can be helpful for students who struggle to start the writing process. Answer b is incorrect because proofreading programs can review what students have written. Answer d is incorrect because word-prediction programs can help predict what a student may want to write.

136. D: Although there are many methods and strategies to use while co-teaching, both teachers need to be present for them to be effective. If the teachers are sharing duties and one teacher is planning, it will be difficult to ensure that each student understands the content. Both teachers need to be involved and on the same page; otherwise, some students will lack the support they need. Answer a is incorrect because both teachers teaching as a team can be a great way to reach every student in the class. Answer b is incorrect because station teaching can be beneficial in that each teacher can teach to their strengths. Answer c is incorrect because it can be beneficial for one teacher to teach their area of specialty while the other teacher supports the students who are struggling.

137. C: Before evaluating him for special education services, it is best to see if his struggles are related to his lack of English skills or if he might have a disability. Testing him right away makes it difficult to make that determination without putting some interventions in place. It is best practice to wait and see what steps need to be taken first. Answer a is incorrect because English learners are eligible for special education services if they are determined to be eligible. Answer b is incorrect because he may or may not have a disability at all. Answer d is incorrect because although it may take him a while to learn the curriculum, this is not necessary in order to evaluate a student for special education.

138. D: Internalization of behaviors tends to have the greatest impact on a student as they change who they are on the outside and the inside. Although this could potentially be positive or negative behaviors, internalizing them makes the deepest impact. Psychology research shows that internalization changes who a person is both on the inside and the outside. Answer a is incorrect because simply conforming to beliefs may not change who a person is on the inside. Answer b is incorrect because complying with their wishes likely will not last very long. Answer c is incorrect because changing their identity may or may not change who they are on the inside.

139. A: A classroom with rows of desks allows the support personnel to move up and down the aisles to support students. This way, they are able to easily access each one of the students. It is important that students that require support have access to that support person, who can help them if needed. Answer b is incorrect because having clusters of desks may make it difficult to access individual students. Answer c is incorrect because having desks in circles may also make it difficult to work with students. Answer d is incorrect because having long tables also limits this access.

140. D: Although all of these are examples of executive functioning skills that can be beneficial for students to learn, not all of them can be accomplished within a day. Students with ADHD may struggle to attend to attention for long periods of time so daily objectives must be clear and focused. It is important that a daily objective is something that can be attained in a single day. Answer a is incorrect because using a planner independently is likely a skill that will take more than a day. Answer b is incorrect because memorizing the state capitals would likely take weeks. Answer c is incorrect because although sitting silently without talking may be something that can be accomplished in a day, it is not likely to be a skill that improves executive functioning abilities.

141. B: It is likely going to be most beneficial to pull Greg from one of his classes once a week so he understands what he is going to be working on and how it will be implemented. For students who struggle with social skills, it can be helpful to first work in a small setting to practice the skills rather than in a large class. It is important not to overwhelm these students or make them feel uncomfortable considering their needs. Answer a is incorrect because pulling him from class every day likely would be too frequent in that he would miss a lot of class. Answer c is incorrect because implementing this intervention into general education right away might not be as effective because Greg may not know what is expected of him. Answer d is incorrect because it may be difficult to implement an intervention that is not within school hours.

142. B: In order to use technology to meet the needs of all kinds of learners, it is important to allow students some freedom to learn using the method that meets their needs. When students are able to access their peers, they can learn using a variety of methods including collaboration. This allows the students to work with each other in a variety of ways while using the tablet, which may include videos, articles, and other types of projects. Answer a is incorrect because a slide show presentation likely will only target a certain group of students in the class. Answer c is incorrect because audiobooks may be beneficial to some students but not to others. Answer d is incorrect because simply giving them computers may not be productive for each student in the class to work independently.

143. C: The most appropriate probe for a curriculum-based assessment in the area of written expression for a second grader would be to write a paragraph. Curriculum-based assessments are designed to see what a child is able to do by challenging them but giving them something that can be accomplished at a certain point. Writing paragraphs is something that students in second grade are likely working on or striving toward, which is why this probe would be beneficial for Jadon. Answer a is incorrect because second graders likely do not know how to write an essay yet. Answer b is incorrect because although spelling may be helpful, being able to compose sentences tends to be more valuable. Answer d is incorrect because writing one sentence likely does not provide quite enough information.

144. C: Portfolios can be a beneficial assessment tool in many ways including accessing how much progress a student has made over a period of time. This can include a collection of writing samples, probes, or any other activity that can be measured. This can often be a more accurate measure of student growth for students with disabilities that struggle with traditional exams. Answer a is incorrect because determining what a student knows at the end of a unit would be a formative assessment. Answer b is incorrect because determining a student's interests would be an interest inventory rather than a portfolio. Answer d is incorrect because comparing a student to their peers would be considered a norm-referenced assessment.

145. D: For students who struggle with behavior, it is often helpful to have someone in the classroom to help support the general education teacher. In order to ensure inclusion for students, it is important that they have access to the general education curriculum as often as possible. Having a paraprofessional in the class to support the student allows them to access the curriculum and have support when they need it. Answer a is incorrect because although placing a student with a specific teacher can be helpful, support should still be in place no matter who the teacher may be. Answer b is incorrect because if a student is constantly pulled from the classroom, they will miss the instruction. Answer c is incorrect because although teaching him strategies can help, it may be more beneficial for him to be in the class learning with his peers.

146. A: The family of students who receive special education services must be provided a copy of their procedural safeguard rights, according to IDEA. These safeguards allow the family to know and understand what they can do if they have questions or concerns about the services that their family member may be receiving. These are important in establishing the ground rules of special education laws and services. Answer b is incorrect because the procedural safeguards do not provide families access to educational records. While federal laws such as FERPA do give families the right to access these records, this is not a right given by the federal safeguards notice or IDEA. Answer c is incorrect because although schools must provide prior written notice, this is separate from the procedural safeguard rights. Answer d is incorrect because the school is not required to provide an independent educational evaluation.

147. B: The calculator is considered mid tech because it is an example of a device that requires technology but does not typically need to be plugged in or require much maintenance. Calculators are typically used for students who struggle with math calculations and require extra support in the classroom. This kind of assistive technology can be beneficial in that it does not require much more than carrying the calculator to class. Answer a is incorrect because low-tech assistive devices would include everyday items such as pencil grips and graphic organizers. Answer c is incorrect because high-tech assistive devices would include devices that require more maintenance including text-to-speech software and tablets. Answer d is incorrect because no-tech devices are not considered assistive technology, but the calculator is because it is a device that helps a student access the curriculum.

148. B: One of the most productive ways to prevent a student from misbehaving in class is to express what the expectations and ground rules for the class will be. Preventive strategies are designed to handle the misbehavior before it happens. Students who struggle with following directions will likely need to learn the rules of the class early on in order to try and limit this behavior. Answer a is incorrect because modeling how to follow directions likely would be ineffective as a preventive strategy if the behavior has already occurred. Answer c is incorrect because giving the student consequence choices would not be considered preventive because it has already happened. Answer d is incorrect because meeting with the student to discuss the behavior would also not be considered a preventive strategy and rather a reaction to the behavior.

149. B: Formative assessments are designed to measure student progress while the students are learning in order to gauge what they can do. These tend to be more informal assessments that are not associated with a grade. Formative assessments can be beneficial for students with disabilities in guiding what level of support they may need as instruction moves on. Answer a is incorrect because the assessment before the instruction would typically be the diagnostic. Answer c is incorrect because the summative assessment typically occurs after the learning has been completed. Answer d is incorrect because it is most beneficial for students to give them a formative assessment during their learning in order to guide instruction.

150. A: Although there tends to be a high number of children with disabilities in foster care, it is not quite as high as being the majority. However, children that are in the foster care system do tend to have a much higher chance of having a disability. According to FindLaw.com, one third of children in foster care suffer from a disability. Answer b is incorrect because when students are unable to find placement, many times their disability worsens, and their condition deteriorates. Answer c is incorrect because children in foster care have often suffered from abuse. Answer d is incorrect because it can often be difficult for children with disabilities to find a permanent home.

Practice Test #2

1. Cory is a 10th-grade student with an other health impairment due to ADHD. Which one of the following social influences is likely to have the most impact on his academic performance?

   a. The education levels of his parents
   b. The composition of his household
   c. His race or ethnic background
   d. The friends he spends time with

2. Justin is a ninth-grade student with a specific learning disability in the area of reading comprehension. Which of the following strategies would be most effective in ensuring that he maintains his knowledge of a story?

   a. Asking him to read the story three times in a row
   b. Asking him to reread the story for homework
   c. Asking him to reread the story each week
   d. Asking him to quiz himself on the story

3. Grace is a fourth grader who receives special education services as a student with an autism spectrum disorder. Which of the following is not true about Grace and accessing the alternate assessment?

   a. Grace would access the alternate assessment if she requires substantial modification.
   b. Grace would access the alternate assessment if she requires intense individualized instruction.
   c. Grace would access the alternate assessment if she cannot access a pencil-and-paper test.
   d. Grace would access the alternate assessment if she displays difficult behavior.

4. Which of the following best describes the purpose of the Education for All Handicapped Children Act of 1975?

   a. To mandate FAPE for students with disabilities
   b. To provide grants to states to fund special education programs
   c. To establish services to facilitate school-to-work transitions
   d. To allow students with disabilities to be included in statewide assessments

5. Which of the following is most likely to be true about students with learning disabilities and their families?

   a. Families that have children with disabilities typically bond closer.
   b. Parents can sometimes be the cause of a learning disability.
   c. Parents will often suspect a disability before the school does.
   d. Families often seek out information about disabilities.

6. Lori is a 10th-grade student with a postsecondary goal of becoming an artist. Which of the following would likely be most productive in helping Lori reach this goal?

   a. Setting up an appointment with the art teacher at school
   b. Giving her a list of schools to research
   c. Having her call local art galleries in town
   d. Allowing her to take an online vocational test

7. The Vineland Adaptive Behavior Scales would be most appropriate to administer to which of the following students?
    a. A student with an emotional disturbance
    b. A student with a development delay
    c. A student with an intellectual disability
    d. A student with a specific learning disability

8. Which of the following pieces of special education legislation implemented the child find process for students who are suspected of having disabilities?
    a. Education for All Handicapped Children Act of 1975
    b. Individuals with Disabilities Education Act of 1990
    c. Individuals with Disabilities Education Act of 2004
    d. Elementary and Secondary Act of 2001

9. Which of the following strategies would be least effective in structuring an inclusive classroom environment?
    a. Providing multisensory approaches to learning
    b. Maintaining a structured routine
    c. Developing clear rules and expectations
    d. Using station learning opportunities

10. Corey is a second-grade student who receives special education services due to a specific learning disability in the area of reading fluency. Which of the following is the best strategy for ensuring success for Corey if he is severely impacted by his reading fluency deficiencies?
    a. Providing additional support in the classroom
    b. Pulling Corey for small-group reading fluency intervention
    c. Modifying the material that Corey is to complete
    d. Pulling Corey for one-to-one reading fluency intervention

11. Which of the following best describes how often at minimum a behavior intervention plan should be updated?
    a. Once a year at the annual IEP meeting
    b. Each time the student has a new teacher
    c. On every progress report date
    d. As the IEP team deems it necessary

12. Which of the following is the best example of how to interpret the results of a diagnostic assessment?
    a. To determine the instructional level that students are at
    b. To determine the disability that a student may have
    c. To determine the kind of special education services that a student needs
    d. To determine the amount that a student has learned

13. Javier is a fourth-grade student with an emotional disturbance. Which one of the following individuals is least likely to be a member of his IEP team?
    a. School psychologist
    b. Director of special education
    c. Student
    d. School principal

14. Which of the following strategies is likely to be most effective in overcoming any kind of personal cultural biases when working with students with disabilities?
   a. Learning about why the cultural bias takes place
   b. Being objective when evaluating these students
   c. Treating each of the students the same way
   d. Encouraging cross-group participation among peers

15. Which of the following is true about stakeholder rights and an Independent Educational Evaluation (IEE)?
   a. The testing is administered by someone who works outside of the school district.
   b. The IEP team must accept the results of the IEE.
   c. The parents must pay for the IEE to be conducted.
   d. The parents must explain the reason for the IEE.

16. Andrea is a first-grade student with a developmental delay. How can a formative assessment be implemented to monitor her progress throughout the school year?
   a. Interviewing her each week
   b. Giving her academic probes
   c. Observing her in class
   d. Monitoring her test scores

17. Which of the following is a disadvantage to having special education teachers support classrooms rather than co-teach?
   a. Special education teachers do not have as much time to plan.
   b. Special education teachers are not as familiar with the content.
   c. Special education teachers cannot differentiate instruction.
   d. Special education teachers must collaborate with classroom teachers.

18. Which of the following is true of co-occurring conditions for students with ADHD who receive special education services?
   a. Anxiety is the most common co-occurring disorder for students with ADHD.
   b. Speech problems are more common in students without ADHD.
   c. Almost half of students with ADHD also have a learning disability.
   d. The majority of students with ADHD have conduct disorders.

19. Which of the following instructional strategies is most appropriate when lecturing to a class that includes students with disabilities in a high school class?
   a. Giving the students access to the presentation
   b. Giving the students skeleton notes to fill in
   c. Giving the students an exemption from taking notes
   d. Giving the students a partner to take notes with

20. Which of the following best describes the most effective use of a developmental assessment?
   a. As a norm-referenced scale
   b. As a quick identifier
   c. As a behavior rating scale
   d. As an alternate assessment

21. Which of the following pieces of information is typically not required during the prereferral process for special education?

   a. Parental consent
   b. Data
   c. Monitoring
   d. Strategy discussion

22. Which of the following is true about discipline and students who receive special education services according to IDEA?

   a. A manifestation determination must be held after 10 days of suspensions.
   b. Students with disabilities cannot be suspended more than 10 days.
   c. Discipline for special education students is the same as general education.
   d. Special education services are not provided for expelled students.

23. Which of the following best describes one of the goals of a behavior plan?

   a. To increase behaviors
   b. To diagnose behaviors
   c. To correct behaviors
   d. To challenge behaviors

24. Which of the following classroom arrangements would be most appropriate for active teaching and learning?

   a. Traditional rows and columns
   b. Horseshoe shape
   c. Clusters
   d. Runway seating

25. Which of the following is an example of a fine motor skill that a four-year-old student would be expected to do?

   a. Hop on one foot
   b. Catch a ball
   c. Cut with scissors
   d. Ride a tricycle

26. Jordan is a fifth-grade student with an intellectual disability who is given a behavior rating scale assessment. Which of the following best describes how the results of adaptive behavior scales can benefit Jordan?

   a. To determine which accommodations a student may need
   b. To decide whether or not modifications are appropriate
   c. To develop a behavior intervention plan
   d. To incorporate functional skills in his lesson

27. Which one of the following strategies is likely to be the most beneficial for at-risk students with disabilities who struggle with mental illness?

   a. Offering to seek help from the student's parents
   b. Asking questions to seek more information
   c. Allowing them to be alone with their feelings
   d. Informing the school counselors of the concerns

28. Which of the following best describes the goal of implementing a functional curriculum for students with disabilities?
   a. To teach independent living skills to students
   b. To teach communication skills to students
   c. To teach basic subjects to students
   d. To teach everyday tasks to students

29. When working with a group of eighth-grade students with writing deficiencies, which of the following intervention strategies would be most appropriate?
   a. Providing a graphic organizer for the students to use
   b. Modeling the writing for the students
   c. Providing opportunities for the students to practice
   d. Allowing students to collaborate with peers

30. Which of the following intervention strategies would be most effective in assisting a student who struggles to learn vocabulary terms?
   a. Providing them with a multisensory model
   b. Supplying visuals with the words
   c. Creating frequent vocabulary quizzes
   d. Allowing students to use a dictionary

31. Jared is a fifth-grade student with Down syndrome. Which of the following co-occurring conditions is Jared most likely to suffer from over the course of his life?
   a. Heart diseases
   b. Traumatic brain injuries
   c. Diabetes
   d. Depression

32. Which of the following is not one of the dispute-resolution processes that a parent or stakeholder may choose for a child with a disability who receives special education services?
   a. Filing a complaint with the Department of Education
   b. Asking for a mediation to find a compromise
   c. Filing a due process complaint
   d. Removing the student from the school

33. Which of the following strategies would be most appropriate for creating a supportive learning environment for students with emotional disturbances?
   a. Ensuring that everyone in the class speaks their opinion
   b. Pairing students together to share their experiences
   c. Asking probing questions to open up the discussion
   d. Collaborating with the students to set group parameters

34. Which one of the following does not describe the use of behavior rating scales?
   a. To obtain judgments of a student's behavior in a standardized format
   b. To screen students to obtain information about specific behaviors
   c. To monitor the progress of students with severe behavior concerns
   d. To classify students as having psychological problems

35. Ross is a third-grade student who receives special education services as a student with an other health impairment due to ADHD. Which of the following strategies would likely be least effective for Ross?
   a. Providing extra think time when asking a question
   b. Providing one-on-one math instruction
   c. Providing a setting with fewer distractions
   d. Providing a model to demonstrate the task

36. When determining the continued eligibility for a student with a specific learning disability, which of the following tests would be most appropriate to administer?
   a. Intelligence test
   b. Achievement test
   c. Screening test
   d. Curriculum-based test

37. Which of the following is the best description of maintaining a previously learned skill?
   a. Performing the skill in a variety of settings
   b. Practicing the skill when it is learned
   c. Progressing on the learned skill
   d. Continuing to practice the learned skill

38. Which of the following instructional strategies would be most effective for students who access computer-assisted instruction?
   a. Supplementing their online instruction with face-to-face instruction
   b. Assisting them in seeking support from their online teacher
   c. Providing opportunities to demonstrate the knowledge learned online
   d. Providing accommodations for their online learning

39. Which of the following is the best example of an independent living skills goal for a high school student with a specific learning disability?
   a. The student will be able to access the city bus.
   b. The student will live with a roommate in an apartment.
   c. The student will live in a group home.
   d. The student will attend community college.

40. Which of the following students would most likely benefit from community services as part of their postsecondary transition goals?
   a. Students with autism spectrum disorder
   b. Students with emotional disturbances
   c. Students with multiple disabilities
   d. Students with traumatic brain injuries

41. Which of the following community services would be most appropriate for a group of high school students with specific learning disabilities?
   a. Job skills trainers
   b. Independent living agencies
   c. College recruiters
   d. Mental health services

42. Which of the following characteristics would be the least common in students who receive special education services under the multiple disabilities category?
    a. Hampered speech and communication skills
    b. Challenges with mobility
    c. Assistance with everyday tasks
    d. Loss of vision and hearing

43. Which of the following is the most productive instructional strategy when working with at-risk learners with disabilities?
    a. Allowing the students to access accommodations
    b. Providing a caring classroom setting
    c. Allowing these students to collaborate with peers
    d. Providing opportunities for after-school activities

44. Which of the following is a criticism of the humanism learning theory?
    a. The theory does not account for internal influences.
    b. The theory does not consider the social aspect of learning.
    c. The theory is relative and does not provide right or wrong answers.
    d. The theory does not clearly define inherent goodness.

45. According to IDEA, which one of the following areas is not considered when determining eligibility for the developmental delay category?
    a. Fine motor development
    b. Cognitive development
    c. Language development
    d. Personal development

46. Which of the following best describes the implications for teaching for those who follow the behaviorist learning theory?
    a. The teacher communicates through positive or negative reinforcements.
    b. The teacher provides an environment that promotes self-learning.
    c. The teacher facilitates collaborative learning and group work.
    d. The discovery of students' behavior is guided by the teacher.

47. Which of the following checks for understanding would be most appropriate when teaching a small-group writing lesson to seventh graders?
    a. Using white boards
    b. Using self-assessments
    c. Using cooperative learning
    d. Using flip charts

48. Which of the following best describes how technology can be included in a small group of students with disabilities working on reading comprehension?
    a. Accessing audiobooks to listen to the story
    b. Using computers to research the author of the story
    c. Accessing speech-to-text software to answer questions
    d. Using tablets to read a story and answer questions

49. How can a summative assessment be implemented for students with disabilities?
   a. Monitoring their progress on IEP goals
   b. Asking them to complete a portfolio at the end of a unit
   c. Evaluating them for continued eligibility
   d. Diagnosing which accommodations they need

50. Which of the following agencies would likely be most appropriate for high school students with specific learning disabilities?
   a. School-to-work agencies
   b. Independent living agencies
   c. College counseling agencies
   d. Military recruiting agencies

51. Which of the following is the best example of guided practice when supporting a fifth-grade general education social studies class with multiple students with disabilities?
   a. Students independently complete a map worksheet.
   b. Teachers provide feedback on the map worksheet.
   c. Students work in small groups to complete the map worksheet.
   d. Teachers model how to complete the map worksheet.

52. Brittany is a four-year-old preschool student who is administered a developmental assessment as part of her special education evaluation. Which of the following disability categories would least likely be considered as a result of these assessments?
   a. Development disability
   b. Speech or language impairment
   c. Specific learning disability
   d. Autism spectrum disorder

53. How might a lesson introduction be most beneficial when teaching students with learning disabilities about math?
   a. To provide students with additional information
   b. To ensure that students understand the curriculum
   c. To connect the learning from the previous lesson
   d. To challenge the students to learn as much as possible

54. When teaching an eighth-grade class, which one of the following strategies in communicating with parents best promotes a safe classroom environment?
   a. Sending home the list of class rules to the parents
   b. Getting to know the background and interests of the parents
   c. Ensuring that behavior issues are communicated to parents
   d. Reporting positive student behavior to the parents

55. Brian is a 12th-grade student with an intellectual disability. Which of the following would be the best example of a functional curriculum in his science class?
   a. Learning how to conduct an experiment
   b. Learning how to read a book about planets
   c. Learning how to maintain a garden
   d. Learning how to calculate speed

56. Which of the following is true about the Family Education Rights and Privacy Act and students with disabilities?

   a. Each teacher in the school has access to the student's IEP.
   b. Schools are not required to allow parents to inspect previous IEPs.
   c. Previous IEPs can be amended at any time.
   d. Parents have the right to access testing protocols.

57. Chad is a fifth-grade student with ADHD who needs active involvement to stay focused, but who enjoys being away from people. How can the use of a workspace in the corner of the class be best implemented in the classroom to be beneficial for Chad?

   a. Chad can be sent to the corner when he becomes disruptive.
   b. Chad can go to the corner when he has an assignment to work on.
   c. Chad can go to the corner to reward good behavior after he finishes his work.
   d. Chad can go to the corner when he needs a break.

58. In order for students to make progress on their IEP goals, which of the following makes the most sense when grouping students for a math intervention group?

   a. Grouping students based on their ability level
   b. Grouping students based on their grade level
   c. Grouping students based on their teachers
   d. Grouping students based on their maturity level

59. Which of the following disability categories would a student with a developmental disability most likely be eligible for under IDEA?

   a. Emotional disturbance
   b. Autism spectrum disorder
   c. Speech or language impairment
   d. Specific learning disability

60. Marie is a fifth-grade student who receives special education services as a student with a hearing impairment. Which of the following sections in the IEP describes the support that Marie will receive specific to her disability?

   a. Communication plan
   b. Annual goals
   c. Accommodations
   d. Special factors

61. Which of the following strategies is most effective in measuring the goals of students with behavior concerns?

   a. Using curriculum-based measures
   b. Comparing students to their peers
   c. Counting the number of referrals
   d. Using random time samples

62. Jacob is a third-grade student who scored one standard deviation below average in written expression on an academic achievement test. Which of the following best describes the likely next step for Jacob?

   a. Jacob will be determined eligible for special education services.
   b. Jacob will need additional tests specific to written expression.
   c. Jacob will need to be administered an intelligence test.
   d. Jacob will need to be evaluated for special education services.

63. Jessica is a ninth-grade student who struggles with becoming distracted while she works in the general education setting. Which of the following methods of differentiated instruction would be most beneficial to Jessica?

   a. Differentiating the learning environment
   b. Differentiating the content
   c. Differentiating the process
   d. Differentiating the product

64. Which one of the following is not typically used to collect data as a curriculum-based assessment?

   a. DIBELS
   b. AIMSweb
   c. EasyCBM
   d. TerraNova

65. Which of the following is least likely to be the responsibility of an elementary school special education teacher?

   a. Communicating accommodations to general education teachers
   b. Managing the schedules of paraprofessionals
   c. Team-teach lessons in the classroom setting
   d. Facilitation of 504 plans and meetings

66. Cheyenne is an eighth-grade student with an other health impairment due to a heart condition, and she struggles with attendance. Which of the following would be the best example of a weekly objective in assisting Cheyenne in getting caught up?

   a. Cheyenne will talk to each of her teachers at the beginning of each week.
   b. Cheyenne will meet with her case manager to develop a plan in getting caught up.
   c. Cheyenne will come in before school to talk to her teachers.
   d. Cheyenne will complete all of her missing assignments by the end of the week.

67. When teaching a classroom with students with disabilities, which of the following would be most effective in building self-esteem?

   a. Starting with material that is easy for them
   b. Being patient with their learning needs
   c. Allowing students to work in groups
   d. Using positive nonverbal communication

68. Which of the following activities would be considered atypical cognitive development for a four-year-old?
   a. Making up words and stories
   b. Drawing pictures of objects
   c. Pretending to read and write
   d. Pointing to objects they want

69. Which one of the following learning environments best allows for differentiated instruction?
   a. Randomly placing the students with additional support needs throughout the classroom
   b. Selectively placing the students with additional support needs throughout the classroom
   c. Placing the students with additional support needs clustered together
   d. Placing the students with additional support needs at the front of the class

70. Which of the following best describes when it would be appropriate to provide one-on-one in-class support to a fifth-grade student who receives special education services and has been demonstrating an inability to attend to his general education teachers?
   a. As soon as the student demonstrates these behaviors
   b. At the student's annual IEP meeting
   c. After data have been collected and analyzed
   d. When the student gets suspended from school

71. Which of the following instructional strategies is most appropriate in supporting the transition goals of eighth-grade students?
   a. Researching professions that they may be interested in
   b. Researching colleges that they may want to attend
   c. Researching classes that the high school offers
   d. Researching independent skills that they may need

72. Which one of the following is the best example of a culturally responsive special education classroom?
   a. Acknowledging ethnic holidays and celebrations
   b. Pairing students with similar backgrounds
   c. Incorporating texts from various cultures
   d. Showing popular films from different cultures

73. Sasha is a kindergarten student who seems to be struggling with the curriculum in her class. Which of the following screening tests would be least likely to benefit Sasha before determining whether or not a special education evaluation is appropriate?
   a. Communication screening
   b. Hearing and vision screening
   c. Motor skills screening
   d. Cognitive screening

74. David is a fourth-grade student who has been struggling with some of his behaviors. Which of the following frequent behaviors would be most concerning when observing David?
   a. Using swear words with peers
   b. Bragging to gain attention
   c. Telling lies and being dishonest
   d. Having disagreements with friends

75. Which of the following classroom organization methods would be most beneficial for a teacher who includes a lot of classroom discussions?
   a. Including a meeting area in the classroom
   b. Arranging the desks facing toward each other
   c. Having tables instead of desks
   d. Ensuring that each student can move around

76. Dustin is a ninth-grade student who struggles with his organizational skills. Which of the following assistive technology devices would be most beneficial in helping him improve these skills?
   a. FM listening systems
   b. Speech recognition programs
   c. Data managers
   d. Abbreviation expanders

77. How would the use of a supplementary curriculum be most appropriate for a group of high school students in a social studies class?
   a. Providing the students with accommodations to access the curriculum
   b. Providing the students opportunities to explore careers
   c. Providing the students use of assistive technology
   d. Providing the students extra credit for additional assignments

78. Braden is a 10th-grade student with a specific learning disability. Which one of the following examples best describes when the results of his standardized testing may be unreliable?
   a. If Braden did not test at the appropriate instructional level
   b. If Braden did not access his accommodations
   c. If Braden did not take the alternate assessment
   d. If Braden did not receive proper instruction

79. Shamus is an eighth-grade student with a specific learning disability in the area of written expression. Which of the following is the best example of a curriculum-based measure to monitor his progress in this area?
   a. Giving him a story starter and counting his writing sequences
   b. Giving him a list of spelling words to memorize and spell
   c. Giving him a class period to construct an essay
   d. Giving him a picture and asking him to write a sentence

80. Which of the following does not describe one of the methods that students with disabilities can use to access the general education curriculum?
   a. Changing the content that they are taught
   b. Changing the method in which they are taught
   c. Changing the demonstration of what they are taught
   d. Changing the environment in which they are taught

81. Which one of the following environmental factors is likely to have the greatest impact on students who receive special education services due to mental health concerns?
   a. Sleep deprivation
   b. Smoking
   c. Exposure to toxins
   d. Substance abuse

82. Jeffrey is an eighth-grade student with a deficiency in reading fluency. Which of the following assistive technology devices would be least appropriate in supporting his needs?
   a. Text-to-speech device
   b. Speech-to-text device
   c. Audiobooks
   d. Graphic organizers

83. Which of the following is the most important reason for students with disabilities to generalize a learned skill?
   a. To be able to use different materials
   b. To be able to work with different people
   c. To be able to use skills in multiple settings
   d. To be able to expand on previous knowledge

84. When evaluating a sixth-grade student for a specific learning disability, which one of the following is an academic achievement test that can be administered?
   a. CogAT
   b. Woodcock-Johnson
   c. Iowa Test of Basic Skills
   d. Scantron

85. Zachary is a 10th-grade student who receives special education services as a student with an other health impairment due to his ADHD, and he struggles to sit still for long periods of time. Which of the following strategies would be most effective in providing opportunities for Zachary to move around?
   a. Giving Zachary a pass to move around when he needs to
   b. Giving Zachary a timer to get up and stretch every 10 minutes
   c. Organizing the classroom so that Zachary has his own area
   d. Incorporating movement activities for the entire class

86. Which of the following would be the best example of a learning objective that is appropriately challenging for a third-grade student with a disability in reading fluency?
   a. The student will be able to identify 25 letters in one minute.
   b. The student will be able to identify 25 letter sounds in one minute.
   c. The student will be able to read 50 sight words in one minute.
   d. The student will be able to read 100 words in one minute.

87. Which of the following would be the least appropriate reason to provide a social skills intervention group for students?
   a. To teach social problem solving
   b. To teach behavioral skills
   c. To decrease antisocial behaviors
   d. To increase friendships

88. Which of the following is not one of the components of a free appropriate public education (FAPE)?
   a. Parents must participate in IEP meetings.
   b. Schools must provide the best possible education.
   c. Schools must notify parents of changes to the IEP.
   d. Parents are allowed to request an outside evaluation.

89. Jaden is a second-grade student with a diagnosis of ADHD. When conducting a special education evaluation, which of the following behavior rating scales would be most appropriate?
   a. Single-domain scales
   b. Self-report scales
   c. Multidomain scales
   d. Observer/informant scales

90. Which of the following lifelong skills can be incorporated into a writing intervention group for eighth-grade students?
   a. Email writing
   b. Essay writing
   c. Letter writing
   d. Résumé writing

91. Which of the following least describes when the co-teaching model would be effective for teaching an English lesson to a group of seventh-grade students?
   a. To increase the amount of attention that students receive
   b. To share control over the classroom
   c. To increase the amount of differentiation
   d. To provide multiple areas of expertise

92. Which of the following is not true with regard to English learners receiving special education services?
   a. There are no tests to definitively rule out learning disabilities.
   b. They typically exhibit a disability in their native language first.
   c. They must have adequate learning before a determination can be made.
   d. Background knowledge can be a factor in the determination.

93. Which of the following best explains why learning objectives should be time-bound?
    a. Objectives should explain the progress toward achievement.
    b. Objectives should require a reasonable amount of resources.
    c. Objectives should lead to a desired goal.
    d. Objectives should include a date in relation to the accomplishment.

94. Which of the following is the most appropriate use of technology to provide assistance with reading a story for a high school student who struggles with reading comprehension?
    a. Allowing the student to use text-to-speech programs
    b. Allowing the student to watch videos of the stories
    c. Allowing the student to complete an online activity
    d. Allowing the student to complete an electronic worksheet

95. Which of the following is the best example of how a student with a specific learning disability can access standardized tests?
    a. Allowing them to access alternate tests
    b. Allowing them to access modified tests
    c. Allowing them to access accommodated tests
    d. Allowing them to access differentiated tests

96. Madison is a third-grade student who receives special education services due to a hearing impairment. Which of the following special services providers would be least likely to attend her reevaluation meeting?
    a. Speech-language pathologist
    b. Occupational therapist
    c. School nurse
    d. District audiologist

97. Which of the following is not required as a component of an IEP?
    a. Accommodations
    b. Objectives
    c. Annual goals
    d. Present levels

98. Which of the following is not true about the referral process for special education eligibility?
    a. Parental consent is required to start the evaluation.
    b. The evaluation must be completed in 30 days.
    c. The evaluation must be conducted by a multidisciplinary team.
    d. The referral may be initiated by a parent.

99. Ricky is a seventh-grade student being evaluated for special education services who is administered an IQ test. Which of the following best describes the results of his test if he scored a 100?
    a. Ricky scored in the average range.
    b. Ricky got all of the questions correct.
    c. Ricky does not need special education services.
    d. Ricky does need special education services.

100. Jimmy is a general education eighth-grade student who is starting to struggle in the area of math calculations. Which of the following is the next step for his teacher?
   a. Referring Jimmy for special education services
   b. Attempting accommodations inside the classroom
   c. Contacting Jimmy's parents about getting a tutor
   d. Offering to work with Jimmy after school

101. Which one of the following circumstances is least likely to impact the family of a child with a disability?
   a. The type of condition that a student has
   b. The severity of the condition that a student has
   c. Knowledge of the family about disabilities
   d. The financial wherewithal of the family

102. Which of the following examples is least likely to be considered a formative assessment technique?
   a. Analyzing student work
   b. Strategic questioning
   c. Unit pretests
   d. Exit tickets

103. Jessie is a fourth-grade student with an emotional disturbance. Which of the following behavior management models would be most likely to meet his needs?
   a. Assertive discipline
   b. Logical consequences
   c. Reality therapy
   d. Love and logic

104. Which of the following is the most advantageous in implementing small-group pull-out instruction for high school students with disabilities?
   a. Providing students access to their IEP accommodations
   b. Allowing the students to ask questions
   c. Ensuring that the students are making progress on their goals
   d. Strengthening their knowledge of reading, writing, and math

105. Tristan is a 10th-grade student with a specific learning disability in the area of reading comprehension. Which of the following examples would likely be the most beneficial in administering summative assessments to students like Tristan?
   a. Administering alternate assessments
   b. Administering assessments with modifications
   c. Administering assessments with accommodations
   d. Administering informal assessments

106. Why is instructional scaffolding a useful strategy when teaching students with disabilities?
   a. Students are provided an alternate method of learning the lesson.
   b. Students are provided multisensory approaches to learning the lesson.
   c. Students are provided additional support in learning the lesson.
   d. Students are provided less instruction when learning the lesson.

107. Which one of the following challenges is least likely to arise when collaborating with parents at IEP meetings?
   a. Differences with regard to IEP goals
   b. Differences with regard to accommodations
   c. Differences with regard to attendance issues
   d. Differences with regard to service delivery

108. Which of the following best describes the role of the special education teacher in the multitiered system of supports (MTSS) process?
   a. To provide input on students with disabilities
   b. To discuss students who may need to be evaluated
   c. To provide interventions for students
   d. To discuss students who exit special education

109. Which of the following is not considered a disability category according to IDEA?
   a. Multiple disabilities
   b. Developmental disabilities
   c. Intellectual disabilities
   d. Orthopedic impairment

110. Gordon is a seventh-grade student with an intellectual disability. Which of the following is likely most important in ensuring that Gordon has a meaningful learning experience in the class?
   a. Linking the content to real-life experiences
   b. Making the content student-centered
   c. Promoting self-knowledge
   d. Using a variety of resources

111. Jose is a fourth-grade student who was recently determined to be eligible for special education services. Which of the following strategies would be most beneficial in supporting his family?
   a. Providing them with fact sheets about his disability
   b. Holding informational meetings regularly
   c. Allowing them to shadow his classes
   d. Giving them a list of outside providers

112. Which of the following strategies would likely be most beneficial in preparing a student with a specific learning disability for adulthood?
   a. Incorporating a postsecondary goal in the student's IEP
   b. Incorporating money management skills in the student's class
   c. Incorporating transition services into the student's IEP
   d. Incorporating job application writing in the student's class

113. Which of the following best describes the purpose of state standardized tests?
   a. To compare a student's academic achievement to a norm
   b. To determine how much progress a student has made
   c. To find strengths and weaknesses in a student's development
   d. To determine the intellectual ability of students

114. Which of the following best describes how daily learning objectives can be implemented to assist students who are working on adaptive skills?
   a. To teach students to learn how to complete a new task
   b. To teach students to improve reading ability
   c. To teach students to learn about organization
   d. To teach students to improve basic math skills

115. Gerald is a fifth-grade student with a deficiency in reading fluency. How can the results of a diagnostic assessment in this area help to guide his instruction?
   a. To figure out how much progress Gerald has made
   b. To help decide which areas to focus on the most
   c. To compare Gerald to his peers in the class
   d. To understand which accommodations will work for Gerald

116. Which of the following best describes alternate assessments and students that receive special education services?
   a. Most students who receive special education services take alternate assessments.
   b. Students that take alternate assessments do not receive high school diplomas.
   c. Parents have the option to choose whether students take alternate assessments.
   d. Alternate assessments are not based on grade-level standards.

117. Which of the following strategies can a special education teacher implement to best ensure that inclusion is successful in their school?
   a. Articulating the need for inclusion to the school administrators
   b. Collaborating with general education teachers
   c. Developing new assessments to measure student growth
   d. Providing professional development to staff

118. Which of the following is least likely to explain the gender gap in identification of boys and girls for learning disabilities?
   a. Boys are born with a higher tendency to develop a learning disability.
   b. Boys are referred for evaluation more often due to a behavior bias.
   c. Many tests are standardized for use with boys.
   d. Expectations tend to be higher for girls.

119. When working with students who struggle with managing their own behavior, which of the following would not be considered a positive behavior intervention?
   a. Social-emotional strategies
   b. Consequences
   c. Self-regulatory strategies
   d. Coping skills

120. Which of the following best describes how an intelligence test can guide instruction?
   a. To determine whether or not a student has an intellectual disability
   b. To determine whether a student has an emotional disability
   c. To determine which accommodations students should access
   d. To determine whether a student has a learning disability

121. Which of the following would be the most effective communication strategy when working with a student who has frequent misbehaviors due to his disability at school?

   a. Sending home a weekly behavior report
   b. Asking general education teachers to contact parents
   c. Asking the school psychologist to contact parents
   d. Sending home a daily behavior report

122. Which of the following best describes how math simulation assistive technology can help students with disabilities access the curriculum?

   a. Assisting students in recognizing the text
   b. Assisting students in writing the problems
   c. Assisting students in hearing the text
   d. Assisting students in conceptualizing the problem

123. Jeanine is a ninth-grade student who often disrupts class with outbursts when she doesn't get her way. Which of the following would be the least effective in managing her behavior when this occurs?

   a. Ignoring her
   b. Calling for backup
   c. Engaging with her
   d. Removing her from class

124. Marissa is an 11th-grade student who accesses special education services as a student with autism spectrum disorder. Which of the following lesson plan elements would likely be most beneficial in meeting her needs in her math class?

   a. Providing a cross-curricular curriculum
   b. Providing multiple tasks to complete
   c. Providing multiple choices
   d. Providing hands-on instruction

125. Which of the following best describes how students who receive special education services are also protected under Section 504 of the Rehabilitation Act of 1973?

   a. Students who receive special education services also receive 504 plans.
   b. Students who exit special education must receive 504 plans.
   c. Students with 504 plans also receive special education services.
   d. Students who graduate high school can access 504 plans in college.

126. Which of the following best describes one of the roles of the special education paraprofessional in a middle school setting?

   a. Toileting students with disabilities
   b. Collaborating with general education teachers
   c. Communicating with parents
   d. Attending IEP meetings

127. Which of the following learning theories views motivation as extrinsic and intrinsic?

   a. Behaviorism
   b. Cognitivism
   c. Constructivism
   d. Humanism

128. When developing a lesson plan for a small group of students with specific learning disabilities in the area of writing, which one of the following is most important?
    a. Ensuring that the students are accessing their accommodations
    b. Ensuring that the students are working on their IEP goals
    c. Ensuring that the students have access to the general education curriculum
    d. Ensuring that the students have access to an alternate curriculum

129. Parker is a sixth-grade student who receives special education services as a student with a specific learning disability. Which of the following responsibilities would the special education teacher most likely perform in assisting Parker?
    a. Monitoring the progress of his IEP goals
    b. Providing mental health support
    c. Ensuring he has access to modifications
    d. Providing executive functioning interventions

130. Which one of the following disability categories is likely to have the greatest impact on individuals across their life span?
    a. Developmental disabilities
    b. Speech or language impairments
    c. Multiple disabilities
    d. Specific learning disabilities

131. Which of the following best describes the purpose of the prior written notice section of the IEP?
    a. To invite parents to the IEP meeting
    b. To provide copies of rights to parents
    c. To propose changes to the IEP
    d. To end special education services

132. Which of the following best describes when it would be necessary for a teacher to create their own assessment?
    a. When students do not have access to the curriculum
    b. When testing students with intellectual disabilities
    c. When providing accommodations to students
    d. When the academic standards are modified

133. Bobby is an 11th-grade at-risk student with a specific learning disability who rarely sees either of his parents. Which of the following instructional strategies is likely to be most effective for Bobby long term?
    a. Helping Bobby research colleges he might want to attend
    b. Giving Bobby extra support to pass all of his classes
    c. Teaching Bobby executive functioning skills
    d. Assisting Bobby in applying and interviewing for jobs

134. Anna is a fourth-grade student with a disability who is struggling with reading comprehension in her social studies class. Which of the following would be the best option for ensuring that Anna can appropriately access the general education curriculum?
 a. Moving Anna to the third-grade social studies class
 b. Reteaching the concepts in her special education class
 c. Placing a paraprofessional in her social studies class
 d. Modifying the content in her social studies class

135. Which of the following is the best example of how nonverbal communication can be used to manage student behavior?
 a. Looking at students when they misbehave
 b. Posting classroom rules and policies
 c. Smiling at a student when they behave
 d. Including visual aids to improve content delivery

136. Which of the following issues would be most likely to arise when teaching a large group of students with a wide range of disabilities?
 a. The teacher may not be able to meet the student's IEP goals.
 b. The teacher may not be able to provide accommodations.
 c. The teacher may not be able to incorporate assistive technology.
 d. The teacher may not be able to appropriately differentiate.

137. Which of the following is an example of an early intervention service for a student who is being evaluated for a developmental disability?
 a. Speech services
 b. Academic services
 c. Counseling services
 d. Adaptive services

138. Rob is a second-grade student with a hearing impairment. Which of the following characteristics would not be included in the criteria for his continued eligibility?
 a. His hearing impairment is fluctuating.
 b. Amplification improves his hearing.
 c. He also has a visual impairment.
 d. His educational performance is adversely affected.

139. Which of the following is the most appropriate example of differentiated instruction when teaching a math lesson to fourth-grade students?
 a. Creating learning stations
 b. Interviewing students
 c. Targeting different senses
 d. Assigning projects

140. Which of the following is true after a student with a disability graduates from high school?
 a. They can no longer access their IEP.
 b. They can no longer access accommodations in college.
 c. They can no longer access disability services.
 d. They can no longer access accommodations in the workplace.

141. Which of the following wouldn't be considered a social environmental factor that could potentially impact students with disabilities?
   a. Poverty
   b. Loss of a parent
   c. Poor nutrition
   d. Family discord

142. Alex is a ninth-grade student who receives services as a student with a traumatic brain injury. In order to be eligible to receive services under this disability category, which of the following causes of the injury can be ruled out?
   a. Birth trauma
   b. Combat injuries
   c. Violence
   d. Sports-related injuries

143. Which of the following is not one of the benefits of using curriculum-based assessments?
   a. To measure short-term student growth
   b. To match the classroom curriculum
   c. To inform a teacher's instruction
   d. To motivate students to improve

144. Which of the following best describes the difference between a 504 plan and an IEP?
   a. IEPs last through postsecondary education, whereas 504 plans end after high school.
   b. IEPs contain services and accommodations, whereas 504 plans only contain accommodations.
   c. IEPs are governed through the Rehabilitation Act and 504 plans through IDEA.
   d. IEPs come from the Office for Civil Rights, whereas 504 plans are through the Department of Education.

145. Which of the following would least likely be one of the responsibilities of the school psychologist with regard to providing support for students with disabilities?
   a. Providing mental health support
   b. Administering IQ tests to students
   c. Training staff on behavior plan implementation
   d. Facilitating IEP meetings

146. Which of the following best describes how classroom centers can be appropriate for students with disabilities?
   a. Centers can be beneficial in personalizing the instruction.
   b. Centers can be beneficial in providing individual instruction.
   c. Centers can be beneficial in providing different levels of instruction.
   d. Centers can be beneficial in allowing for group instruction.

147. Which one of the following is the best example of cooperative learning when teaching a class that contains a mix of students with disabilities and the general education population?
   a. Student-selected teams
   b. Heterogeneous teams
   c. Random teams
   d. Homogeneous teams

148. Which of the following best describes the use of a screening test for struggling students?
   a. To determine eligibility for special education services
   b. To determine whether an in-depth assessment must be conducted
   c. To determine a student's progress on IEP goals and objectives
   d. To determine which classes a student should take

149. When screening a student for potential deficiencies as a preschooler, which of the following would be considered typical emotional development?
   a. Changing the rules of a game they play
   b. Being rigid with daily routines
   c. Wanting to be dependent on caregivers
   d. Struggling to take turns with peers

150. Matthew is a third-grade student with an emotional disturbance who struggles with outbursts. Which of the following observation methods would be most beneficial when conducting a formative assessment?
   a. Tally marks
   b. Time sampling
   c. Qualitative observations
   d. Verbatim scripting

Answer Key and Explanations

1. B: Although all of these choices can have positive and negative impacts, the composition of a household can have a strong impact either way. Children who come from a household in which both parents are present and supportive can have a huge impact on the access they have to educational support. Children who have little support in the home or come from broken homes have a high chance of struggling academically. Answer a is incorrect because although education levels of a student's parents can be a factor, it is more important to the student the support they are able to provide. Answer c is incorrect because although a person's race or ethnic background can have a major impact, their home life will likely influence them more. Answer d is incorrect because the friends a person spends time with likely will not impact the student as much as how they were raised.

2. C: When maintaining a skill, it is important to practice that skill periodically over the course of time. For someone that struggles with reading comprehension, it is important to practice reading multiple times to ensure that the content is remembered. Students with disabilities who struggle in certain areas will likely need extra practice for maintaining these skills. Answer a is incorrect because simply reading the story a few times in a row will not allow the student to maintain the skill long-term. Answer b is incorrect because just rereading the story once for homework likely will not allow him to maintain the skill either. Answer d is incorrect because although quizzing himself may be a valuable strategy in helping him remember the story, it likely will not allow him to maintain this skill.

3. D: Students would typically not access the alternate assessment simply for displaying poor behavior. Alternate assessments are designed for students who cannot access the general standardized assessments due to low cognitive functioning rather than behavior functioning. Although students with behavior concerns may need accommodations to access the general assessment, they can still access it. Answer a is incorrect because students that need substantial modification to the curriculum typically access the alternate assessment. Answer b is incorrect because students that need intense individual support would also have a difficult time accessing the standard assessment. Answer c is incorrect because students that cannot access a pencil-and-paper test also need to access the alternate assessment, which is often computer-based.

4. A: The Education for All Handicapped Children Act of 1975 established that children with disabilities must be provided FAPE. This law became the basis for all special education funding and services through the federal government. The establishment of FAPE was important for students with disabilities and continues to be today. Answer b is incorrect because grants to states to fund special education programs had already been established prior to the passage of this act. Answer c is incorrect because school-to-work facilitation legislation was passed after 1975. Answer d is incorrect because the inclusion of all students with disabilities in statewide testing also occurred after the passage of this legislation.

5. C: Although all of these choices may be true in certain situations, parents of students with disabilities will typically see some of the signs before the child is evaluated at school. The parents spend a good deal of time with these children, so they are aware of what they can and can't do. They may not know for certain whether or not a student has a disability, but they can determine what they struggle with at home. Answer a is incorrect because families of children with disabilities are more likely to experience issues than they are to come together. Answer b is incorrect because parents are not the cause of the learning disability and also cannot be the cure. Answer d is incorrect because families do not often seek this information out to learn more about disabilities.

6. A: Although all of these choices may be beneficial to certain students, setting up an appointment with the school's art teacher will allow her to get some information from an artist. This will allow her to see what options she may have to choose from and which paths she could potentially go down. Discussing this information with someone who has likely been in a similar situation can help to provide clarity and direction for students. Answer b is incorrect because simply researching schools may or may not help her narrow down what her plan and goal might be. Answer c is incorrect because just talking to employees at local art galleries may not provide much information about becoming an artist. Answer d is incorrect because although a vocational test might be helpful, it won't give her much specific information about paths to go down.

7. C: Adaptive behavior scales such as the Vineland Adaptive Behavior Rating Scales are typically designed for students with intellectual disabilities who struggle with personal and social skills. Although these scales can be used for students who receive services in other disability categories as well, students with intellectual disabilities can benefit the most. These plans can be helpful in determining how a student functions at school and at home in order to best support the students. Answer a is incorrect because students with emotional disturbances likely do not exhibit the deficits needed to take these assessments. Answer b is incorrect because students with developmental delays may or may not benefit from these assessments, but they tend to be given to older students. Answer d is incorrect because students with learning disabilities typically do not display these deficits.

8. C: The Individuals with Disabilities Act of 2004 established the child find process in order to identify students with disabilities starting from an early age. This process required schools to locate and evaluate students suspected of having a disability, no matter how severe or impactful it may be. This legislation was important in establishing a process to identify these students and provide the support they may need access to. Answer a is incorrect because the Education for All Handicapped Children Act of 1975 ensured that services were provided to students who already had disabilities. Answer b is incorrect because the Individuals with Disabilities Act of 1990 was implemented to provide the same opportunities for students with disabilities as those without. Answer d is incorrect because the Elementary and Secondary Act of 2001 was implemented to close student achievement gaps for all students.

9. B: Although some students may thrive in a structured routine, it is important for the teacher to be open to change and being flexible. It is possible that lesson plans or teaching strategies don't go as planned, so it is important for the teacher to be able to change the routine when needed. Students with disabilities will especially need flexibility in the teacher meeting their needs on a daily basis. Answer a is incorrect because every student in the class can benefit from a multisensory approach. Answer c is incorrect because developing clear rules and expectations allows the students to understand what they can and cannot do in the class. Answer d is incorrect because station learning can allow students to work with peers and learn using a variety of techniques.

10. D: Although all of these choices may benefit Corey to a certain extent, providing one-to-one intervention in reading fluency is most likely to improve his reading fluency. One-to-one instruction allows Corey to move at his own pace and move on to the next skill when he has mastered the previous skill. This allows the teacher to truly meet Corey's needs in reading fluency and give him complete attention during the intervention time. Answer a is incorrect because a student with a severe deficiency in reading fluency likely needs additional intervention outside the classroom. Answer b is incorrect because a small group would not allow Corey to work at his own pace and provide the individual instruction that he may need. Answer c is incorrect because modifying the material will not allow Corey to build his reading fluency skills.

11. A: A behavior intervention plan is required to be updated at least once a year at the annual IEP meeting. Although there is no timeframe for when the behavior intervention plan must be implemented other than the annual IEP meeting, it is important to monitor. When students exhibit new behaviors or change behavior patterns, it might be time to make an update. Other students may not need updates more than once per year. Each student has different needs, and it is vital that each member of the team takes part in monitoring the student and their plan.

12. A: Although diagnostic assessments may be helpful in determining each of these choices, they can most often be used to discover what a student's instructional level is. Diagnostic assessments are typically given before the instruction in order to determine what level that a student is at. This may mean changing their class or providing additional support or interventions depending on the student. Answer b is incorrect because the diagnostic assessment alone would not be able to determine what disability a student may have. Answer c is incorrect because although the diagnostic can assist in determining the special education services for a student, it likely would not be the only measure used. Answer d is incorrect because a summative assessment would be more appropriate to determine how much a student has learned.

13. C: Students in elementary school do not typically attend their IEP meetings. These students are often too young to attend and understand the discussion at the meeting, so they are most often not invited to the meeting. It is important to understand a student's maturity level before inviting him or her to an important meeting to discuss their IEP. Answer a is incorrect because the school psychologist can be an important member of the IEP team for students with emotional disturbances in writing behavior plans or monitoring goals. Answer b is incorrect because the director of special education is also often invited to these IEP meetings. Answer d is incorrect because most school districts require a building administrator to attend IEP meetings as well.

14. A: Although all of these strategies can be beneficial in overcoming cultural biases, learning why the bias occurs is likely to be the most effective. If teachers are able to analyze and understand why some of the biases occur, they may be able to eliminate them or overcome them. Cultural biases occur for many reasons, but it is important to understand the impact that a teacher has and what the needs of the student might be. Answer b is incorrect because being objective may not be quite as effective as showing empathy for certain students. Answer c is incorrect because not all students will likely learn the same way so they should not necessarily be treated the same. Answer d is incorrect because simply encouraging these cross-group interactions may or may not help in overcoming personal biases.

15. A: When parents request an IEE, the testing must be administered by someone that does not work for the same school district. Parents have the right to request an IEE when they do not agree with the results of a special education evaluation. The school must consider the results of this evaluation in order to ensure that it is providing FAPE. Answer b is incorrect because although the IEP team must consider the results of the evaluation, they do not have to accept them. Answer c is incorrect because the school district is required to pay for the IEE. Answer d is incorrect because an explanation is not required for the parents to request an IEE.

16. C: Although all of these choices may be examples of some kind of formative assessment, observing her in class is most likely to provide the best data. Formative assessments are designed to assess what the student knows as the learning occurs. In order to monitor progress using formative assessments, it is important to take a look at the areas the student struggles in and if she is improving. Answer a is incorrect because interviewing a first grader like Andrea may not always provide the most accurate data. Answer b is incorrect because giving her academic probes most likely would not show whether or not she is developing on her social and behavioral skills. Answer d is incorrect because simply monitoring how she does on tests may not provide the whole picture in how she is developing overall.

17. B: Although there are many pros and cons to co-teaching, one of the advantages is that both teachers are familiar with the content and can plan together. When special education teachers are supporting the general education classroom teachers, they do not have this opportunity. This can cause special education teachers to be lost and supporting students in content they are not familiar with or experts in. Answer a is incorrect because special education teachers will likely still have the same amount of time to plan either way. Answer c is incorrect because special education teachers have the opportunity to differentiate instruction in either one of these models. Answer d is incorrect because collaborating with classroom teachers should be used in every method when assisting students with disabilities.

18. C: It is very common for children with ADHD to also exhibit learning deficiencies in one or more areas. These students will often struggle to attend to their education, which causes them to fall behind and struggle with their learning. It is important to recognize and understand which disabilities a student may struggle with. Answer a is incorrect because learning disabilities are the most common co-occurring conditions with ADHD. Answer b is incorrect because speech problems tend to be more common in students with ADHD. Answer d is incorrect because fewer than half of students with ADHD also have conduct disorders.

19. B: Although all of these choices may be beneficial in certain situations, it is most helpful to provide students with skeleton notes so they can keep up with the lecture and take notes. Many students with disabilities struggle to keep up with the pace of a typical lecture, so this strategy can allow them to understand the content and also write the notes. Note-taking is a valuable skill, so allowing them to practice it while also comprehending the lecture is valuable. Answer a is incorrect because simply giving them the entire presentation may overwhelm these students and create more work. Answer c is incorrect because giving them an exemption may cause them to lose focus or not pay attention to the lecture. Answer d is incorrect because it may not always be appropriate to have a partner during lecture time.

20. A: Developmental assessments are designed to find strengths and weaknesses in young students who may be exhibiting some delays. In order to do this, students are compared with what the average student is capable of doing in many developmental categories. These assessments can be effective in intervening in students early who may be struggling. Answer b is incorrect because a quick identifying assessment that would be used is typically referred to as a screener. Answer c is incorrect because a behavior rating scale typically identifies just the behavior of students of all ages. Answer d is incorrect because an alternative assessment is typically used for students with disabilities who cannot access standardized tests.

21. A: During the prereferral process, parents are not typically required to give their consent. This process typically consists of identifying areas in which the student struggles and developing strategies to assist this student. This may consist of interventions inside or outside of the classroom in addition to accommodations or modifications. Answer b is incorrect because it is important to collect data to determine whether or not a student is making sufficient progress. Answer c is incorrect because monitoring is important because it determines whether or not new strategies need to be implemented to better meet student needs. Answer d is incorrect because constantly evaluating the strategies and discussing them as a team is a necessary component of the prereferral process in meeting student needs.

22. A: After students with disabilities have been suspended for 10 days over the course of a school year, a manifestation hearing is scheduled to determine whether or not the behavior is a manifestation of the student's disability. This is to ensure that the student is not being disciplined simply because they have a disability. If the behavior is not a manifestation of the student's disability, then they will receive the same punishment as any other general education students. Answer b is incorrect because these students can be suspended for more than 10 days if it is not a manifestation of their disability. Answer c is incorrect because discipline may be different depending on the manifestation results. Answer d is incorrect because services can still be provided to students who get expelled from school.

23. A: One of the main goals of behavior plans is to increase certain behaviors that students may not be exhibiting. Students that struggle with participating in the class or social group may need a behavior plan that is targeted at increasing participation in the class. It is important to identify not only students who exhibit negative behaviors but also students who do not exhibit positive behaviors. Answer b is incorrect because the behavior plan is not designed to diagnose behaviors but rather to develop a plan for what to do when these behaviors occur or do not occur. Answer c is incorrect because the behavior plan does not correct behaviors; rather, it reinforces the behavior that the student is working on. Answer d is incorrect because the behavior plan does not challenge any behaviors.

24. C: Although all of these arrangements may have their benefits for certain students, clusters easily allow students and teachers to work together and move from group to group. Active teaching and learning is a beneficial strategy in that the students get to move around and work with different students. This cluster arrangement allows this movement for all students, including those with disabilities who may need to be accessed quickly and easily. Answer a is incorrect because traditional rows and columns tend to be more teacher-centered and do not allow for much movement throughout the room. Answer b is incorrect because although the horseshoe shape can provide space for the teacher to move, it doesn't provide as much freedom for the students. Answer d is incorrect because runway seating tends to be beneficial for teacher movement, but the students wouldn't be able to move as much.

25. C: A typical four-year-old would be expected to start cutting paper with scissors. This is an example of a fine motor skill because it is a skill that uses small muscles such as those of the hands and fingers rather than large muscles. It is important to recognize the difference between fine and gross motor skills in order to determine which may be age appropriate or could potentially be a deficit. Answer a is incorrect because hopping on one foot uses larger muscles groups so it would be an example of gross motor skills. Answer b is incorrect because catching a ball also would be considered an example of gross motor skills. Answer d is incorrect because riding a tricycle also involves the larger muscle groups in the legs.

26. D: Adaptive behavior scales are designed to measure personal and social skills of individual students. These are typically designed for students with intellectual disabilities in order to determine what they are capable of accomplishing. The results of these scales can determine what students need to improve both inside and outside of the classroom. Answer a is incorrect because although these may help guide the accommodations a student may need, they are more likely used to understand what a student can do and what they need extra help with. Answer b is incorrect because these scales typically do not evaluate whether or not modifications are appropriate for students. Answer c is incorrect because a functional behavior assessment would be more appropriate in determining whether a behavior plan would be beneficial.

27. D: Although each student may react differently to this support, it is important to seek help when it is warranted. Students that have or are suspected of having mental illnesses should be kept under a watchful eye, and help should be sought as soon as possible. For these students, it may be necessary to seek support from the school counselors even if the student is unaware. Answer a is incorrect because at-risk students may or may not want their parents to know about their concerns and this may trigger some strong emotions. Answer b is incorrect because asking too many questions might make these students feel uncomfortable. Answer c is incorrect because leaving them alone may not be productive if they are struggling and need some support.

28. A: Although all of these choices may be beneficial to students with disabilities, a functional curriculum is designed to teach students independent living skills. This curriculum typically replaces traditional secondary curriculum for certain students who may be candidates at the high school level. It tends to be designed for students who will struggle to live independently once they complete their schooling. Answer b is incorrect because although it may be helpful in developing communication skills, the sole purpose is not just for this communication development. Answer c is incorrect because functional curriculum is an alternative curriculum rather than teaching the basic subjects. Answer d is incorrect because functional curriculum focuses more on skills that will apply after high school rather than current everyday tasks.

29. A: Although all of these choices may be beneficial to certain students, providing a graphic organizer will likely produce the best long-term results. A graphic organizer can be beneficial for students who struggle with organizing their writing in that it gives them a framework for how to set it up. Many students struggle to organize their writing and stay on topic, and the graphic organizer is designed to help with this. Answer b is incorrect because simply modeling the writing likely is not enough support for many students. Answer c is incorrect because just providing opportunities to write without any feedback will not allow much improvement for the students. Answer d is incorrect because although collaboration can be helpful in certain circumstances, giving students the tools to complete work independently will help develop their writing skills.

30. B: Students tend to remember vocabulary words when they have some kind of visual to associate with what the word means. Many students that struggle with vocabulary words often need a lot of practice in understanding these new words, so giving them multiple methods to learn the words is beneficial. Simply telling the students what words to memorize often does not work with students with disabilities that struggle with vocabulary. Answer a is incorrect because providing a multisensory model may be helpful for some students but this is more of a strategy that is used for reading fluency. Answer c is incorrect because additional vocabulary quizzes might become too overwhelming for some students. Answer d is incorrect because although a dictionary can help learn the term at first, this strategy will not likely be effective in the long term.

31. A: More than half of individuals born with Down syndrome also suffer from heart conditions throughout their lifetime. Although many of these develop when they are born, heart conditions can arise at any time. This can lead to high blood pressure and an inability to get blood pumped to the heart. Answer b is incorrect because although traumatic brain injuries can happen in individuals with Down syndrome, they are most often caused by external factors and can happen to anyone. Answer c is incorrect because although diabetes is often diagnosed in those with Down syndrome, heart diseases are the most common. Answer d is incorrect because depression and mental health issues do not have quite the impact that heart conditions do.

32. D: Although removing the student from the school is certainly an option, this is not typically one of the dispute-resolution processes. These processes are designed for parents to work through disputes that they may have with their child's IEP in order to find a solution. Removing the student from the school likely would not solve the problem with regard to the IEP. Answer a is incorrect because parents and stakeholders have the right to file a complaint with the Department of Education if they choose to. Answer b is incorrect because asking for mediation can be a beneficial way to seek a compromise in regard to the IEP. Answer c is incorrect because parents can also file a due process complaint if the other two strategies prove to be unsuccessful.

33. D: Although all of these strategies may be beneficial to certain students, those with emotional disturbances often are reluctant to share information. It would be valuable to hear their input on the expectations and parameters of the class in order to get an idea of what they might be comfortable with. They would be more likely to share their experiences if they helped establish the boundaries. Answer a is incorrect because ensuring that everyone speaks might not make all of the students in the class comfortable. Answer b is incorrect because pairing students in groups may not always be beneficial if the students are not comfortable with each other. Answer c is incorrect because asking probing questions might also be uncomfortable for students.

34. D: Although behavior rating scales can be useful for many reasons, classifying students as having psychological problems is not one of them. Simply using one test to determine whether or not a student has these issues is typically not appropriate. It might be beneficial to use an assessment such as the behavior rating scale as part of a body of evidence in making a determination about a student. Answer a is incorrect because these scales can compare a student with their peers in order to determine appropriate behaviors. Answer b is incorrect because these scales can also be used to screen students for potential problems. Answer c is incorrect because behavior rating scales can help in monitoring the progress of students with severe behavior concerns over time.

35. B: Although all of these instructional strategies can be helpful in allowing students with ADHD access to the general education curriculum, providing small group instruction in certain subjects is not always beneficial. Many students with ADHD will simply need support in the classroom or in a separate setting. It is important to understand the functioning of a student before providing small-group or individualized instruction. Answer a is incorrect because extra think time can allow students to collect their thoughts before they speak. Answer c is incorrect because settings with fewer distractions allow these students to concentrate. Answer d is incorrect providing a model to demonstrate can allow the student to see how something is done before doing it.

36. B: Students with learning disabilities are typically provided achievement tests in order to determine eligibility. Achievement tests assess the academic achievement of students and compare those scores with students of a similar age. Based on the results of these reading, writing, and math tests, it can be determined whether or not there is a discrepancy between a student's score and that of their peers. Answer a is incorrect because intelligence tests are used to determine the cognitive ability of a student rather than what they achieve academically. Answer c is incorrect because a screening test would be used before the achievement test to determine whether achievement testing was necessary. Answer d is incorrect because curriculum-based tests are typically used to monitor the progress of students.

37. D: Maintenance is important in ensuring that students are able to retain the information that they have learned on a particular topic. In order to do this, the students must practice the skill regularly to ensure that it is not forgotten. Depending on the skill, this may mean daily, weekly, or monthly practice in order to maintain what has already been learned. Answer a is incorrect because performing the skill in a variety of settings would be an example of generalization. Answer b is incorrect because simply practicing the skill when it is learned may make it difficult to maintain the skill. Answer c is incorrect because progressing on the skill can be helpful, but this may not necessarily help in maintaining the learned skill.

38. B: Although all of these choices may be beneficial in supporting students who access computer-assisted instruction, helping them seek support is likely the most helpful. Students who take online classes may struggle to understand how to seek help and who to contact if they need it. Having someone to help them find ways to get in touch with the teacher of the course can be extremely helpful, especially for students with disabilities. Answer a is incorrect because simply supplementing the online instruction may give the students more work to complete. Answer c is incorrect because although providing opportunities to demonstrate knowledge can be helpful, it may be difficult without knowing the content of the class. Answer d is incorrect because providing accommodations would be something that should occur because of a student's disability and not as an instructional strategy.

39. B: Although students with specific learning disabilities do not always have independent living skills goals included in their IEP, living with a roommate is a reasonable goal. Independent living skills goals are designed to target an important area of focus for students after they graduate high school. Living with a roommate is often an attainable goal for students with specific learning disabilities. Answer a is incorrect because it likely would not be appropriate for students like this to target riding the bus as a goal. Answer c is incorrect because students with specific learning disabilities are not as likely to live in a group home. Answer d is incorrect because attending community college might be appropriate but would be considered an education goal.

40. C: Although students in each disability category will often access these community services, students with multiple disabilities tend to be impacted the most and have the highest chance of using community services. The community services section of the transition goals is designed for services that will need to be in place for students who struggle to live on their own. Students with multiple disabilities are often impacted to the point that they will have a difficult time living independently and can benefit from services through the community. Answer a is incorrect because although some students with autism spectrum disorder will access community services, this is not always the case. Answer b is incorrect because students with emotional disturbances are impacted in a wide variety of ways and many times, these students do not access community services. Answer d is incorrect because students with traumatic brain injuries are also impacted in many ways, many of which do not result in accessing community services.

41. A: Although all of these choices may potentially be beneficial for students with specific learning disabilities, job skills trainers would likely benefit all of these students. Students with specific learning disabilities will often need to improve their job seeking, interview, and career interest abilities in order to pursue a career after high school. Job skills trainers can help them in each of these areas and provide them with the support they will need to be confident in their career. Answer b is incorrect because the majority of students with learning disabilities will not need independent living assistance. Answer c is incorrect because although many of these students may attend colleges and universities, more will likely attend community colleges and vocational programs. Answer d is incorrect because although many of these students will need mental health services, more will likely benefit from job skills training.

42. D: When students suffer from deafness and blindness, they will receive services under the "deaf-blindness" category, according to IDEA. Students who are just deaf or blind and also have a different disability would be considered under the multiple disabilities category. It is important to consider the impact that a disability has on a student so they can receive the services they need and are appropriately identified. Answer a is incorrect because speech issues are common with students who suffer from multiple disabilities. Answer b is incorrect because mobility issues are common because one of the impairments tends to be physical. Answer c is incorrect because students with multiple disabilities are often impacted to the point where they need assistance throughout their lifetime.

43. B: Although all of these choices can be helpful strategies for students who are at risk, showing them that they are cared for is most likely to be successful. Many of these students do not have much positive support in their lives and need someone that they can trust and rely upon. Although it may be difficult for these students to open up and talk, it is important that they have someone that they can turn to when they need to talk. Answer a is incorrect because simply giving them accommodations may not provide them with enough support to be successful. Answer c is incorrect because many of these at-risk learners may be hesitant to trust or want to work with other students in the class. Answer d is incorrect because providing opportunities for after-school activities may or may not fall within of the duties of a teacher.

44. D: The humanism theory suggests that humans are innately good and have a need to make themselves better. The theory states that human experiences influence the behaviors and decisions they make, but it takes an optimistic approach to the human experience. Although the theory states that each person is inherently good, it does not define what this means or how it is measured. Answer a is incorrect because a lack of internal influences is a criticism of the behaviorism learning theory. Answer b is incorrect because not considering the social aspect of learning is a common criticism of the cognitivism theory. Answer c is incorrect because being relative and not proving right or wrong answers is an example of the constructivism theory.

45. D: Personal development is not one of the categories or subcategories that are considered when determining students' eligibility for services as a student with a developmental delay. Personal development could potentially fall into one of the other categories, but it is not specific enough to evaluate. When considering the developmental delay category, it is important to look at each of the specific types of development. Answer a is incorrect because fine motor skills are important to consider as part of physical development. Answer b is incorrect because it is important to consider cognitive abilities or intellectual development. Answer c is incorrect because language and speech are also considered to be part of communication development.

46. A: The behaviorist learning theory states that the teacher teaches correct behaviors and the students understand them and apply them in the classroom. This theory is based on positive and negative reinforcement in order for students to learn the behaviors. This is important in understanding which techniques and learning theories might be best for certain students as they learn. Answer b is incorrect because the behaviorist theory states that the student is shaped through reinforcement rather than self-learning. Answer c is incorrect because the teacher facilitating collaborative groups is an example of the constructivist learning theory. Answer d is incorrect because the teacher guiding students in understanding the environment is an example of the cognitivism theory.

47. A: White boards can be very helpful for students who struggle with writing to determine whether or not they understand the lesson. These students, who struggle with writing, have an opportunity to show what they learned by writing it in a fun way. It is important to check and see if students are understanding the material in a way that doesn't feel like they are being assessed. Answer b is incorrect because self-assessments may not always provide the best information on how a student is performing. Answer c is incorrect because cooperative learning would likely be more appropriate for larger groups of students to pair up. Answer d is incorrect because flip charts might be better suited for younger students who need visuals to learn.

48. D: Although all of these choices may be beneficial for students who struggle with reading comprehension, using a tablet allows the student to practice reading and answering questions. It is important for students to practice these skills as much as possible in order to improve them. For many students, using a tablet to read a story may yield better results than simply reading the story and taking a quiz or test. Answer a is incorrect because although audiobooks can be a useful accommodation, it would likely be more productive to have students practice the skill of reading independently when focusing on reading comprehension. Answer b is incorrect because although this may be helpful for students, practicing their comprehension skills is likely a better strategy. Answer c is incorrect because speech-to-text software would be more effective for students who struggle with writing.

49. B: One of the most productive strategies for students with disabilities is through a portfolio. A portfolio allows the students to demonstrate what they know at the end of a unit or section in order to assess them. Summative assessments are designed to evaluate what a student has learned over a period of time and provide them with a grade. Answer a is incorrect because monitoring their IEP goals would be an example of a formative assessment. Answer c is incorrect because evaluating their continued eligibility is not for a grade or based on a particular unit. Answer d is incorrect because determining which accommodations students need is typically part of the IEP meeting.

50. A: Although all of these agencies may be beneficial for certain students based on their individual needs, the majority of these students could use assistance in obtaining and maintaining a job. School-to-work agencies can be beneficial in providing opportunities in the community for students to work. Students with learning disabilities often need assistance in getting started in their job searches. Answer b is incorrect because independent living agencies tend to be for students with more impactful disabilities such as intellectual disabilities. Answer c is incorrect because although some areas may have college counseling agencies, they are not common in most places. Answer d is incorrect because although the military may be a good fit for some students, not everyone would benefit from these agencies.

51. C: Guided practice involves students working together or with the assistance of the teacher. The purpose of implementing guided practice into the lesson plan, especially for students with disabilities, is to ensure that they understand the material by guiding them through it. Rather than just asking them to do the work by themselves right away, they can get some support from the teacher or their classmates. Answer a is incorrect because this would be an example of independent practice. Answer b is incorrect because this would be an example of teacher feedback rather than guided practice. Answer d is incorrect because teachers modeling the instruction would still be part of the instruction.

52. C: Developmental delays typically do not include tests that would determine a student eligible for a specific learning disability. Although these developmental assessments are beneficial in determining what a student may struggle with, it is difficult to determine the academic skills of children at such a young age. Specific learning disabilities typically manifest as students have had more instruction in reading, writing, and math. Answer a is incorrect because the developmental disability category is common for preschool students who are struggling in certain developmental areas. Answer b is incorrect because speech or language impairments are also common with preschool students. Answer d is incorrect because students with a diagnosis of autism are often identified in the autism spectrum disorder category as a preschooler.

53. C: For students with learning disabilities in the area of math, it is important to break their learning down to ensure that everything goes together. If they struggled with the previous lesson, they may need some additional instruction before they can move on to the next lesson. It is important that they are instructed at a speed and a level that meet their needs and ensures that there is a smooth connection between topics. Answer a is incorrect because simply providing students with learning disabilities with more information may overwhelm them. Answer b is incorrect because ensuring that they understand the curriculum will likely come as the lesson is being taught and not before. Answer d is incorrect because it may not be appropriate to challenge these students while learning is still occurring.

54. C: Although all of these choices can help in making sure the classroom is a safe environment, reporting student behavior to the parents immediately can be most effective. When students misbehave, this must be communicated to the parents so further action can potentially be taken. If it is not reported home, students may continue with these poor behaviors and put other students at risk. Answer a is incorrect because simply sending home the class rules may not work for every parent and they may not always keep track of them. Answer b is incorrect because although getting to know the background of the parents might be helpful, this may not benefit the safety of the class. Answer d is incorrect because only reporting the positive behavior can help to build a safe classroom, but it is more important to report negative behavior that might be a safety concern.

55. C: Although all of these choices relate to science and can be functional for certain students, learning how to maintain a garden is likely most appropriate for students like Brian. A functional curriculum is designed to provide opportunities for students to work on their independent living skills. Maintaining a garden is a valuable skill that can be helpful for students like Brian to learn and apply once they graduate high school. Answer a is incorrect because although conducting an experiment may be a useful skill to have, it may not be as useful as having a garden. Answer b is incorrect because learning about planets also likely is not as useful as maintaining a garden. Answer d is incorrect because calculating speed may or may not be something that students like Brian need to know after high school.

56. D: According to the Family Education Rights and Privacy Act, parents have the right to access testing protocols that are used to evaluate students for special education services. These protocols are considered educational records and are considered part of the student's file. Because of this, the Family Education Rights and Privacy Act requires that school personnel must make these available to parents upon request. Answer a is incorrect because only teachers and staff that work directly with the student have access to that student's IEP. Answer b is incorrect because parents have the right to review and inspect previous IEPs that they may not have copies of. Answer c is incorrect because once the IEP has been finalized, parents or school staff members cannot go back and finalize IEPs from previous years.

57. C: Offering the corner workspace to reward good behavior, such as active participation in class, is the best way to use a corner workspace. Teachers should be very consistent with implementation of incentives, as reinforcement can backfire if a reward is used incorrectly. Chad usually requires active involvement from the teacher to stay on task, so giving Chad extra space to do work is not likely to be a successful solution. It is important to have a consistent plan for the corner to only be used when Chad is finished with his assignments for the day. Since Chad likely perceives the corner workspace as a reward, it is not a good idea to use it when Chad is disruptive, as it may help to reinforce disruptive behaviors. Similarly, Chad should not be allowed to use the corner whenever he thinks he needs a break, as Chad may try to take advantage of the incentive to avoid doing work.

58. A: Although all of these choices certainly play a factor in how to group students, in order for them to make progress on their IEP goals it is best that they are grouped by ability level. Each student will have different IEP goals and progress toward those goals, so it is important to place students in groups that will allow for this progress. It may be difficult for students to make progress on these goals if they are in small groups in which they are not working at an appropriate instructional level. Answer b is incorrect because grouping students on their grade level may not help them make progress on their IEP goals because students might be at various levels. Answer c is incorrect because simply grouping students based on their teachers also may involve grouping students at various ability levels. Answer d is incorrect because although grouping students based on maturity level might be important, some students with different maturity levels function at different academic levels.

59. B: According to IDEA, students who are determined eligible for services under the autism spectrum disorder category have a developmental disability. Students with developmental disabilities are impacted mentally or physically in many ways and tend to have severe long-term problems. Students with autism are typically impacted by struggling with verbal and nonverbal communication, which impacts their access to education. Answer a is incorrect because although students with emotional disturbances can also have a developmental disability, this would likely place them in the multiple disabilities category. Answer c is incorrect because students with only speech or language impairments have their own disability category. Answer d is incorrect because students with specific learning disabilities are typically impacted by their academic abilities.

60. A: The communication plan is important for students with hearing impairments to describe the services that students like Marie will receive to access the curriculum. The communication plan describes the support available for students and the strategies that are used to communicate with others. The communication plan also lists the devices and assistive technology that these students may access. Answer b is incorrect because the annual goals describe which areas the student will focus on and be monitored in. Answer c is incorrect because the accommodations will list specific supports that will be put in place for the student to access the curriculum. Answer d is incorrect because the special factors section simply lists whether or not the student accesses the communication plan.

61. D: Although all of these methods may be helpful in measuring a student's behavior needs, using random time samples can be beneficial in determining the frequency of the behavior. Random time samples allow teachers to observe the student at various times throughout the day to determine the cause and frequency of these behaviors. This can be measured to determine how much progress the student is making on their goals. Answer a is incorrect because curriculum-based measures tend to be more effective for students with academic goals. Answer b is incorrect because it may be difficult to measure how a student compares to their peers. Answer c is incorrect because simply counting the number of referrals likely does not provide sufficient data.

62. A: Students that score at or below one standard deviation below the average level on an academic achievement test typically display a deficiency in that area. Because of this, a student like Jacob would likely be eligible for special education services as a student with a writing disability. Although the achievement test is just one piece of data that must be considered, a standard deviation below the average is considered a significant deficiency in that area. Answer b is incorrect because it is not likely that he will need additional testing based on these results. Answer c is incorrect because intelligence testing does not indicate whether or not a student has an academic skill deficiency. Answer d is incorrect because the academic achievement test is part of the special education evaluation.

63. A: In order for a student like Jessica to succeed in the general education setting, it is likely best to differentiate the learning environment. One way to do this would be to create a space in the classroom where there are no distractions. This way, Jessica can still access the content of her peers while still being free from distractions that might impact her ability to learn. Answer b is incorrect because differentiating the content would not be appropriate because she can still learn what the other students learn. Answer c is incorrect because differentiating the process would not be appropriate because she can still learn the content in the same way that the other students learn. Answer d is incorrect because differentiating the product would not be appropriate because she can be assessed using the same methods as other students.

64. D: TerraNova is an example of a standardized test rather than a curriculum-based assessment. Curriculum-based assessments are designed to monitor the progress of students regularly, whereas standardized tests are given annually or semiannually to compare students to a norm. It is difficult to monitor the progress of students on their IEP goals if they aren't monitored frequently. Answer a is incorrect because DIBELS is a common curriculum-based assessment that measures a student's abilities in reading. Answer b is incorrect because AIMSweb produces many curriculum-based assessment probes in the areas of reading, writing, and math. Answer c is incorrect because EasyCBM also assesses a student using curriculum-based assessment probes in many subjects.

65. D: Although special education teachers have a variety of roles and responsibilities, facilitating 504 plans is typically not one of them. These plans are often administered by the school counselors or building administrators. Although it is possible that special education teachers are involved in this process in some capacity, it is typically not the expectation. Answer a is incorrect because communicating student accommodations to general education teachers is a crucial responsibility of the special education teacher. Answer b is incorrect because the special education teacher is typically responsible for assisting in developing the schedule for paraprofessionals. Answer c is incorrect because team-teaching lessons with general education teachers is also often a responsibility in ensuring the instruction is differentiated.

66. B: Although it may be difficult to plan when she will be absent from school, it would be beneficial to Cheyenne to have someone such as her case manager support her in this task. Making up work on a regular basis can be difficult to do for anyone, especially an eighth grader with a disability. The case manager can help Cheyenne come up with a plan in working with her teachers and getting her assignments in. Answer a is incorrect because although it may be helpful to have Cheyenne talk to her teachers, it may be an overwhelming task. Answer c is incorrect because coming in before school might be helpful but only if it is arranged in advance with her teachers. Answer d is incorrect because giving her a deadline may overwhelm her and make it difficult for her to complete any of her work.

67. B: Although all of these choices may help in building a student's confidence, being patient and sticking with them can be valuable. Students with disabilities will often struggle with self-esteem and need someone to believe in them and that they can do it. Being patient with them and their needs allows them to make progress at their own pace without any pressure. Answer a is incorrect because if the material is too easy for students, they might not give their best effort. Answer c is incorrect because working in groups might make them think they aren't as smart as some of the other students. Answer d is incorrect because although positive nonverbal communication can be helpful, it may or may not build self-esteem.

68. D: Children at the age of four will no longer just point to the objects that they want in most cases. These children are able to communicate verbally and ask for what they want with words. If a child is still pointing to objects that they want at the age of four, this may indicate some kind of developmental delay. Answer a is incorrect because making up words and stories is considered typical development. Answer b is incorrect because drawing pictures of objects that they see is common with four-year-olds. Answer c is incorrect because pretending is also an activity that comes with the development of a child who is four years old.

69. B: Although it may be easier in some aspects to have all of the students that need additional support together, this might create some issues. It is important to strategically place these students based on their needs and behavior. The teacher must be able to access these students in different ways that promote a safe and supportive classroom. Answer a is incorrect because randomly placing them could potentially create issues with their peers. Answer c is incorrect because if they are clustered together, they may feel singled out for being different from the other students. Answer d is incorrect because just putting them at the front could also isolate them.

70. C: In order to understand why student behaviors have increased or declined, it is important to collect data before making major changes. Providing support to a student one on one is a significant change to the instruction that the student receives, so it should not be implemented until data have been collected on the student. These data might include what times of the day these behaviors arise or what kind of interactions may be involved with certain behaviors. Answer a is incorrect because the behavior may simply be a short-term situation in which the student does not display them consistently. Answer b is incorrect because although it may be a good thing to discuss at the annual IEP meeting, these do not always fall at the same time that changes need to be implemented. Answer d is incorrect because student suspensions do not necessarily dictate the level of support that a student receives in a class.

71. C: Although all of these choices may be appropriate for certain students of varying disabilities, researching the high school offerings would be considered the most appropriate. Students in eighth grade will likely need to understand how to be successful in high school before they can think about anything after that. It is important to understand what a student's long-term goals are, however, in helping to determine what high school classes might be appropriate for them. Answer a is incorrect because simply researching professions may be overwhelming for certain students who aren't sure what they want to do. Answer b is incorrect because researching colleges is likely something that will begin to occur in high school. Answer d is incorrect because although independent skills may be important, this is also likely something that will wait until high school.

72. C: Although all of these strategies may be beneficial at certain times, incorporating texts from various cultures allows students to learn about other parts of the world. It is a good idea to incorporate texts from some of the backgrounds of the students in the class as a way for others to learn more about that student. It is important to make those students from backgrounds that others may not know about feel comfortable in class. Answer a is incorrect because simply recognizing holidays does not necessarily teach students about that culture. Answer b is incorrect because pairing students with similar backgrounds does not teach the other students in the class. Answer d is incorrect because films do not always portray cultures the way a book does and can misconstrue certain aspects of a culture.

73. D: Although it can certainly be beneficial to perform a cognitive screening on students, these typically come a little later than kindergarten. Many students in kindergarten are still developing, so a cognitive screening does not always provide the best results. These screening assessments are designed to determine what areas students are struggling with, but they can only be useful for age-appropriate activities. Answer a is incorrect because communication screenings can be valuable in determining how well students interact with others. Answer b is incorrect because hearing and vision screenings are important in helping to determine the cause of a student's struggles. Answer c is incorrect because many kindergarten students struggle with motor skills, which may impact their ability to learn.

74. C: Students in fourth grade typically do not display frequent lying and dishonesty. Although there may be some small lies from time to time, it is concerning if this becomes a pattern for a child of this age. It is important to recognize these kinds of patterns when observing students in order to determine the cause and potentially seek help if necessary. Answer a is incorrect because fourth graders may start to experiment with swear words. Answer b is incorrect because bragging is also considered a normal behavior for a fourth-grade student who is seeking attention. Answer d is incorrect because having disagreements is something that would be considered typical for a fourth grader.

75. B: For teachers who like to use a lot of discussion in their class, one strategy is to have the desks facing each other. This allows the students to communicate directly to each other and have conversations rather than the teacher doing most of the talking. This can also allow everyone in the class, including students with disabilities, feel needed and included in the group. Answer a is incorrect because most classrooms likely do not have enough space to accommodate a meeting area large enough for multiple students. Answer c is incorrect because although having tables might be helpful, it may be difficult for students to communicate with everyone in the class when they are at a table. Answer d is incorrect because although ensuring that students can move around is beneficial, it is more important that they can communicate with each other.

76. C: Although all of these choices may be beneficial to students who struggle with organizational skills, data managers are the most effective in helping students organize tasks. These data managers allow students to put information on tasks into a system, and the system is instrumental in organizing it for them. Students with executive functioning skills can benefit from these tools in that they have to do less of the organization and management of information. Answer a is incorrect because FM listening devices are typically for students who struggle with hearing. Answer b is incorrect because speech recognition programs are designed for students who struggle with writing texts. Answer d is incorrect because abbreviation expanders are beneficial in helping students that may struggle with word processing.

77. B: Supplementary curriculum is typically designed to provide opportunities for students to explore experiences that they might be interested in after high school. This may look different for each student, but it can be beneficial in providing students opportunities that they may not otherwise have. A supplementary curriculum can be used for all students but is typically designed for students who may need additional support in accessing a job after high school. Answer a is incorrect because supplementary curriculum typically does not simply mean that the students can access their accommodations. Answer c is incorrect because although assistive technology can be involved in supplementary curriculum, it may not always be. Answer d is incorrect because a supplementary curriculum is not meant to create more work for the students.

78. B: Although all of these factors may be taken into consideration, it is important for students to access their accommodations in order for the test to be reliable. If a student like Braden did not have the accommodations that he is entitled to receive because of the impact of his disability, the test will not be reliable. Many students with learning disabilities will have accommodations on standardized assessments such as extended time or oral presentation of the test. Answer a is incorrect because standardized tests do not necessarily align with what the students are learning in the classroom. Answer c is incorrect because the alternate assessment is designed for students who cannot access the typical standardized assessment. Answer d is incorrect because it may be difficult to determine what proper instruction looks like for specific students.

79. A: Giving a student like Shamus a story starter and counting his correct writing sequences is one of the most beneficial curriculum-based assessments. This assessment focuses on many areas including spelling, punctuation, and content of the writing. Students that struggle with writing will often need practice writing short stories such as these, and it is easy to monitor their progress. Answer b is incorrect because simply giving him a list of spelling words only allows the teacher to focus on one area, spelling. Answer c is incorrect because curriculum-based assessments are not designed to take an entire class period. Answer d is incorrect because giving him a picture to write about might be more appropriate for a younger student.

80. D: Changing the environment in which a student is taught does not typically provide a student access to the general education curriculum. If special education students are taught outside the general education setting in a special education classroom, they do not have the same access to the content and to their peers. It is important to provide this access to students as much as possible. Answer a is incorrect because changing the content to meet their needs still provides them access to the same curriculum. Answer b is incorrect because changing the method in which they are taught also provides the same curriculum with a different method. Answer c is incorrect because changing how they demonstrate knowledge is also allowing students to access the general education curriculum in a way that meets their needs.

81. D: Substance abuse can be an extremely detrimental environment factor, especially for those with mental health concerns. Substance abuse can either lead to mental health concerns in family members, or it can be a cause of concern in the student. It is important to understand some of the causes of the concerns that students are reporting in order to intervene as early as possible. Answer a is incorrect because although sleep deprivation can impact students with mental health concerns, it likely does not have the same impact as substance abuse. Answer b is incorrect because smoking is likely to have more of an impact on a person's physical health. Answer c is incorrect because although exposure to toxins can be detrimental to a person's health, it likely has more of an impact on physical health.

82. B: Speech-to-text devices are typically designed for students who struggle with writing rather than reading fluency. These speech-to-text devices are valuable in allowing students to speak what they might be thinking, and that is transferred into text. It is important to understand which technology is valuable and works for each student based on their individual needs and interests. Answer a is incorrect because text-to-speech devices can be beneficial in assisting students that may struggle to read the text without making mistakes. Answer c is incorrect because audiobooks provide students like Jeffrey a way to access the text without having to read it. Answer d is incorrect because graphic organizers can be beneficial in organizing the story for students who may struggle to put together what they have read.

83. C: Although all of these strategies can be beneficial for students learning skills, being able to use them in multiple settings is considered generalizing the skill. Generalization allows students to apply the skills that they have learned across different settings and locations. It is important to provide students with disabilities opportunities to generalize what they have learned so they understand why their learning is important. Answer a is incorrect because using different materials can be important for students but it may not have the same impact of applying the skill in new settings. Answer b is incorrect because working with different people is also important but that does not necessarily generalize the skill. Answer d is incorrect because expanding on previous knowledge is only important if students have a firm grasp of the initial knowledge.

84. B: The Woodcock-Johnson Tests of Achievement can be used to determine a child's academic strengths compared with their peers and to determine special education eligibility. This is a test that can be used for children aged 2 through adulthood. This test includes specific subtests to identify skill deficits in the areas of reading, writing, and math. Answer a is incorrect because a CogAT test is used to test a student's cognitive ability. Answer c is incorrect because the Iowa Test of Basic Skills is a standardized test, which would not be used to determine a student's eligibility for special education services. Answer d is incorrect because Scantron assessments are also not considered achievement tests and are instead standardized tests.

85. D: All students can benefit from movement activities as a method of stimulating their brain, so incorporating this strategy for all students would be the most beneficial. Although it may not always be possible each class period, finding creative ways to get Zachary up and moving with the rest of the class will make him feel less singled out. It is important to develop a plan for when these movement breaks are needed for students like Zachary and how they can be implemented for the entire class. Answer a is incorrect because Zachary may take advantage of the pass system and use it more than he really needs to. Answer b is incorrect because giving him a timer also might become a distraction to Zachary and other students around him. Answer c is incorrect because giving a student his own area might end up making him feel singled out.

86. D: In order to measure reading fluency, it is essential to provide a student with a reading passage and record how many words they can read in one minute. This can help to determine how much progress a student has made and what they may still need to work on. Reading fluency is an important skill for a third grader to practice each day by reading passages and developing a clear understanding of words. Answer a is incorrect because identifying letters is a skill that students typically work on before third grade. Answer b is incorrect because although identifying letter sounds can be important, it is not always the best indicator of reading fluency ability. Answer c is incorrect because simply reading sight words can help reading fluency skills, but it is not a measure of reading fluency by itself.

87. D: Although it may be possible to increase friendships when implementing a social skills group, this is not likely to be the goal of the intervention. Social skills interventions may be appropriate for students who struggle socially for many reasons including exhibiting poor social skills and behavioral struggles. It may not necessarily be appropriate to implement a social skills group simply to provide an opportunity for a student to make friends. Answer a is incorrect because teaching social problem-solving skills can be an effective way to build social skills. Answer b is incorrect because teaching appropriate behavior can be helpful for students who struggle to exhibit reasonable behavior. Answer c is incorrect because decreasing antisocial behaviors can be beneficial to students who struggle to communicate with others.

88. B: Although schools will do everything they can to provide students with disabilities the best possible education, this is not stated in the law. Schools must provide an appropriate education to students with disabilities, but this is not defined and may be different for each student. It is important to ensure that students are receiving FAPE and have access to general education and special education services. Answer a is incorrect because one of the requirements is to have parents be a part of the IEP team discussion. Answer c is incorrect because parents have the right to be informed whenever there are changes made to the IEP. Answer d is incorrect because parents may have an outside evaluation conducted if they disagree with the results of the special education evaluation.

89. A: Although all of these choices may be beneficial in targeting specific student behavior, single-domain scales tend to be most beneficial for students with ADHD. Single-domain scales are designed to assess a specific area of concern such as executive functioning. Many students with ADHD will have one main area of concern that the evaluators will focus on. Answer b is incorrect because self-report scales tend to be more beneficial for older students who can accurately report their behavioral concerns. Answer c is incorrect because multidomain scales may make it difficult to target one specific area of concern in students. Answer d is incorrect because observer/informant scales tend to be for students with multiple areas of concern in order to determine the cause of the behavior.

90. A: Although all of these choices may potentially prove beneficial to students throughout their lifetime, writing emails will be a valuable skill. Even in eighth grade, students will begin to learn how to draft and send emails, which is a skill that will last throughout their lifetime. Students will likely need support in the word usage and specifics of what to write in an email to various people. Answer b is incorrect because although essay writing can be a valuable skill to have in school, it may not translate to the rest of a person's life. Answer c is incorrect because letter writing may not be a skill that people use their entire lives. Answer d is incorrect because eighth grade may be a little young to start working on résumé writing.

91. B: Although sharing control over the classroom may sometimes be a positive, many teachers may struggle to work together to make co-teaching successful. Unless the roles and responsibilities of each teacher are clearly defined, it may be difficult for each teacher to share control of the classroom. It may also be difficult to find time to plan lessons together, which could potentially make it a struggle to have a shared vision. Answer a is incorrect because co-teaching can increase the amount of attention that students receive because there are multiple teachers in the class. Answer c is incorrect because differentiation should be increased in the co-teaching model because one of the teachers in the class is focused on the struggling learners. Answer d is incorrect because typically in the co-teaching model one of the teachers is an expert in the subject area and the other is a special education teacher.

92. B: Students who are English learners do not necessarily exhibit a learning disability in their native language before English. Sometimes the deficit is apparent in one language and not the other, and many times it is apparent in both. It is important to understand the history of each student when making the determination. Answer a is incorrect because there is not one single test that predicts special education eligibility for English learners. Answer c is incorrect because it is imperative that these students receive proper learning before they can be properly evaluated. Answer d is incorrect because where a student was raised and what they know can also be deciding factors.

93. D: In order for objectives to be time-bound, there must be a date that the objective is to be reached. This is important for ensuring that students are making adequate progress in a timely manner. If the objectives are not bound by time, then they cannot be measured. Answer a is incorrect because the progress toward the achievement is considered the measure of the goal. Answer b is incorrect because using a reasonable amount of resources shows how achievable an objective may be. Answer c is incorrect because the use of objectives leading to a desired goal is a component of relevant or realistic objectives.

94. A: Although all of these examples may help students who struggle with reading comprehension, text-to-speech programs are best in allowing the student to access the curriculum. Text-to-speech programs provide students with reading comprehension problems the opportunity to listen to the same story that the rest of the class is reading. It is important to provide students access to the general education curriculum whenever possible. Answer b is incorrect because watching videos of the story won't always give them all of the information that they need in the story. Answer c is incorrect because an online activity may leave out some of what the rest of the class is doing.

Answer d is incorrect because electronic worksheets may be more beneficial after the story has been read.

95. C: For students with specific learning disabilities, it is important that they are able to access standardized tests to determine what kind of progress they are making. In order for them to access these tests, oftentimes they will need to be provided accommodations. These accommodations allow them to access the same test as their general education peers. Answer a is incorrect because alternative tests are typically for students who cannot access the standardized test even with accommodations. Answer b is incorrect because standardized tests do not typically allow modifications to the tests. Answer d is incorrect because differentiation would be an example of something that would be done in a classroom setting rather than on a standardized test.

96. B: Although it is possible that the occupational therapist would provide services to a student with a hearing impairment, this is not typically the case. Occupational therapists often provide support to students who struggle with motor skills in the school setting. Students with hearing impairments may or may not have these needs, and it is important to understand the areas in which students have needs in order to consult with the appropriate service providers. Answer a is incorrect because speech-language pathologists typically assist students with hearing impairments in working on communication skills. Answer c is incorrect because the school nurse is an important member of the team in determining the health care services that the student may need at school. Answer d is incorrect because the audiologist typically conducts the hearing screening to determine the impact of the hearing impairment.

97. B: Although each one of these other components is required to incorporate into IEPs for students with disabilities, objectives are not. Students will often have objectives that go along with their annual goals, but this is not a requirement for each student. It is important to understand when and how to use objectives in an IEP and which students it may benefit. Answer a is incorrect because accommodations are essential in addressing how students will appropriately access the general education curriculum. Answer c is incorrect because annual goals are a required component of the IEP to determine what area the student will focus on. Answer d is incorrect because present levels are necessary to determine how much progress a student has made.

98. B: Special education evaluations are required to be completed within 60 days or parent consent, not 30. Districts are required to comply with the 60-day limit in order to determine eligibility for special education services. It is important to understand that although the evaluation needs to consider all of the needs of the student and be in-depth, it must also occur in a timely manner. Answer a is incorrect because parental consent is required before the evaluation process can begin. Answer c is incorrect because a multidisciplinary team, including special services providers, special education teachers, general education teachers, parents, and the student, must be involved. Answer d is incorrect because a parent can request that their child be evaluated for special education services.

99. A: A score of 100 on a standard IQ test indicates a score that is right in the middle of the average range when compared to students of his age. This indicates that Ricky's intelligence is in the middle of the data and where it is expected to be for someone of his age. This does not necessarily mean that he does or does not need special education services, however, without the results of additional assessments. Answer b is incorrect because a score of 100 is in the middle of the data, not that he scored a 100% on the test. Answer c is incorrect because additional assessments must be conducted to determine his need for services. Answer d is incorrect because Ricky may not need services depending on the results of other assessments.

100. B: Although all of these choices may be helpful for Jimmy, it would be most appropriate for Jimmy's teachers to attempt some accommodations in the classroom. The first step in the prereferral process for special education is to provide additional supports for students inside the general education classroom. If this support is unsuccessful, then it may be a good idea to seek additional support and refer to the special education team. Answer a is incorrect because it is important to attempt interventions to determine how a student would respond before referring to special education. Answer c is incorrect because although a tutor may be helpful for Jimmy, it is best to try some accommodations to see if those are successful. Answer d is incorrect because it may not be appropriate to offer to work with Jimmy after school.

101. C: Although having knowledge of certain disabilities can certainly be helpful, it may or may not have much of an impact on that family. Simply being aware of and understanding disabilities does not necessarily eliminate some of the struggles that may come with them. There are many physical, social, and emotional costs that likely cannot just go away with knowledge. Answer a is incorrect because the type of condition a student has can have a great impact on the family. Answer b is incorrect because the severity of the condition can also be impactful in the kind of care and treatment that the child may need. Answer d is incorrect because a family who is financially stable will likely be able to provide more support to a child who requires it.

102. C: Unit pretests would typically be considered an example of a diagnostic assessment rather than a formative assessment. Formative assessments are designed to assess students as the learning is occurring, rather than before or after. It is important to informally assess the students while learning occurs in order to determine if the instruction needs to be adjusted. Answer a is incorrect because analyzing student work is a beneficial formative assessment in discovering what the students are capable of. Answer b is incorrect because questioning the students as the learning takes place gives the teacher an understanding of what the students know. Answer d is incorrect because exit tickets can allow the students to demonstrate what they have learned and what they still struggle with at the end of a lesson.

103. D: The love and logic behavior management model would likely be most effective for a student like Jessie because they likely need positive attention and reinforcements. The love and logic method allows the student and teacher to have a conversation and work through some of the solutions using loving ways. Students with emotional disturbances sometimes struggle with consequences and following strict rules and regulations. Answer a is incorrect because assertive discipline states that students must follow specific rules. Answer b is incorrect because logical consequences may give negative consequences that these students may struggle to react to. Answer c is incorrect because reality therapy requires that students manage their own behavior, which may be difficult for students with emotional disturbances.

104. A: Although small-group pull-outs can provide opportunities for all of these choices, allowing these students to access their accommodations is most important. These accommodations may include a quiet setting to learn, having texts read to them, or being retaught certain concepts. At the high school level, it is important to provide these accommodations to students so they can access as much of the general education curriculum as possible. Answer b is incorrect because they students should be allowed to ask questions in a large- or small-group setting. Answer c is incorrect because although it may be a good opportunity to monitor goals, these groups are designed to assist students in accessing the curriculum. Answer d is incorrect because strengthening student knowledge in pull-out groups would typically happen with younger students.

105. C: In order to allow a student with a learning disability in reading comprehension to access summative assessments, it is best practice to provide accommodations. Summative assessments are designed to assess what a student has learned at the end of a unit of period of time, so it is important that they are properly assessed. Students with reading comprehension deficiencies, however, will need to access accommodations such as oral presentation of the text. Answer a is incorrect because alternate assessments are typically administered as standardized tests rather than summative assessments. Answer b is incorrect because students with learning disabilities typically do not access assessments with modifications. Answer d is incorrect because informal assessments are typically used for formative assessments.

106. C: Instructional scaffolding can be a useful tool in teaching students with disabilities because it provides extra support to ensure that the students are comprehending the lesson. Many students with disabilities struggle to understand or engage in the lesson that a teacher is giving. Instructional scaffolding helps these students by connecting learning to previous knowledge or easing the students into the new learning. Answer a is incorrect because providing an alternate method of learning would be an example of changing the lesson to meet the needs of the student. Answer b is incorrect because multisensory approaches tend to occur after the lesson has been taught. Answer d is incorrect because students are provided the same amount of instruction when the lesson is scaffolded, just at a slower pace.

107. C: Although parents may discuss some of the issues they have with their child's attendance at the IEP meeting, this is not typically discussed at the meeting. Differences that arise from the IEP meeting will be typically stem from the IEP itself. Because there is no section in the IEP that specifically discusses attendance issues, this is the least likely issue to arise. Answer a is incorrect because it is common for the parents and teacher to have differences with regard to the student's IEP goals. Answer b is incorrect because parents may disagree about some of the accommodations that their child has access to. Answer d is incorrect because some parents may also have differences of opinion regarding the service delivery section of the IEP.

108. B: Although all of these choices may be involved in the MTSS process in some capacity, it is most likely that the special education teacher discusses which students may need to be evaluated for special education services. The MTSS process is designed to provide general education support for students who may be struggling academically, socially, or emotionally. The special education teacher is typically involved in this process to provide input on students who may not be responding appropriately to these interventions and need to be evaluated for special education services. Answer a is incorrect because the MTSS process is not typically designed to provide support for students who are already identified as having disabilities. Answer c is incorrect because the special education teacher typically is not the individual responsible for providing these general education interventions. Answer d is incorrect because although it may be possible that students who exit special education are discussed through the MTSS process, it is more often designed for students who have yet to be evaluated.

109. B: Students with developmental disabilities do not have a separate category and will likely fall under a different disability category according to IDEA. Developmental delay is considered a category for students who are ages three to nine, but this is not officially considered a developmental disability. It is important to understand the different disability categories in order to determine which category best fits the needs of a particular student. Answer a is incorrect because the multiple disabilities category is used for students who are impacted by more than one disability. Answer c is incorrect because the "intellectual disability" category would typically include students with developmental disabilities. Answer d is incorrect because the orthopedic impairment category meets the needs of students with physical disabilities.

110. A: Although all of these strategies may be helpful in creating a meaningful learning experience for Gordon, connecting the content to real-life experiences can have the most value. Students with intellectual disabilities often learn best by practicing the content they learn rather than simply hearing about it. Because of this, applying what they learn will likely be something they remember longer and can take more from. Answer b is incorrect because simply making the content student-centered may not always provide meaning to these students. Answer c is incorrect because promoting self-knowledge would likely be a better strategy for students who can explore opportunities independently. Answer d is incorrect because simply having many resources may not necessarily provide much meaning.

111. B: One of the most effective ways that special education teachers can support the parents of students with disabilities is to make sure that they stay informed. Holding meetings regularly on different topics can give the parents the tools they need to make their own decisions on what might be best for their child. This can also give them an opportunity to speak to other parents with disabled children to discuss strategies that they have used. Answer a is incorrect because just giving them a list of facts likely wouldn't be as meaningful as holding meetings so they can ask questions. Answer c is incorrect because having them come in to shadow their son likely wouldn't help them with strategies they can use at home. Answer d is incorrect because it can be tricky to give them a list of providers without knowing their financial and healthcare situations.

112. B: Although all of these choices would be helpful in preparing these students for adulthood, money management skills would be most likely to translate into life after high school. Students will need to be able to manage money throughout their entire lives. It is important to give them the tools to be successful in navigating specific scenarios in which they will need to manage their money. Answer a is incorrect because simply including a goal will not automatically prepare a student for adulthood. Answer c is incorrect because not all students are eligible for transition services after high school. Answer d is incorrect because although applying for jobs is important, managing money is something that adults do on a daily basis.

113. A: Although standardized tests can have many functions and be used in a variety of ways, they are designed to compare a student's score with what the average student scores. These can be beneficial in determining whether or not a student is keeping up with their peers in academic areas. Students with disabilities will often take the same standardized tests as their peers, but it is important to understand the areas that they struggle in and how to help them. Answer b is incorrect because progress is typically monitored through measures such as curriculum-based assessments. Answer c is incorrect because finding strengths and weaknesses in a student's development is an example of a developmental assessment. Answer d is incorrect because intellectual ability is typically measured using an IQ test.

114. A: Adaptive skills are skills that people use every day in order to function at home, school, or work. There are many skills in caring for oneself and accessing the community that are important to practice and complete in order to demonstrate understanding. When teaching these skills, it is important to provide opportunities to practice these tasks to determine what students have mastered and what skills needs additional work. Answer b is incorrect because although improving reading ability is important, this would likely not be considered an adaptive skill. Answer c is incorrect because learning about organization is not typically a skill that is practiced in isolation when considering adaptive skills. Answer d is incorrect because basic math skills are also not considered an adaptive skill.

115. B: Assessing a student using a diagnostic test in beneficial in providing a baseline score for what the student is able to do. Gerald's baseline score in reading fluency would give the teacher an idea of how fluently he reads and what areas still need to be improved upon. From there, the teacher can develop a lesson plan based on the results of this diagnostic assessment. Answer a is incorrect because it will not be until the instruction has occurred that progress can be measured. Answer c is incorrect because diagnostic assessments typically measure where the individual is rather than comparing them with peers. Answer d is incorrect because a diagnostic assessment likely would not provide information about which accommodations to use.

116. D: Although all of these choices may be true in certain cases, the alternate assessment is not based on any of the grade level standards for students. These alternate assessments are designed for students who are unable to take the general standardized assessments with accommodations. It is important to understand and determine whether or not students with disabilities are able to access the general standardized assessment. Answer a is incorrect because most students who receive special education services take the general assessment. Answer b is incorrect because although many students who take the alternate test do not receive a high school diploma, this is not always the case. Answer c is incorrect because the decision about alternate testing is typically up to the school based on the needs of the student.

117. B: Although all of these choices can be helpful in ensuring that inclusion programs are successful, collaboration between teachers can best help students with disabilities access the general education curriculum. This collaboration can allow teachers to develop lesson plans and strategies to promote student growth. Without this collaboration, students with disabilities may not be as successful in their classes as they otherwise could have been. Answer a is incorrect because just meeting with the administrators may or may not change the inclusion programs at the school. Answer c is incorrect because although new assessments can help to measure growth, these may not always ensure successful inclusion. Answer d is incorrect because professional development in itself likely will not improve the inclusion model.

118. D: Boys are identified with learning disabilities at a higher rate than girls but not likely because expectations are higher for girls. Although some teachers may have biases and expectations for girls and boys, there is no evidence to suggest that this had led to underidentifying girls. It is, however, important to identify students for special education evaluations for the right reasons. Answer a is incorrect because studies have shown that boys are born with a higher likelihood of developing a disability. Answer b is incorrect because boys tend to exhibit more negative behaviors in the classroom, and these can lead to special education referrals. Answer c is incorrect because studies have shown that some of the tests are standardized for boys and do not always take girls into consideration.

119. B: The use of consequences would be considered a negative behavior intervention because it is a reaction to a student's poor behavior. Positive behavior interventions typically include strategies for the student to use when they might be experiencing frustration. These tend to be strategies for the student or teacher to use before the event takes place, rather than after. Answer a is incorrect because social-emotional strategies can be beneficial in helping the student to stay calm in certain situations. Answer c is incorrect because self-regulatory strategies can also help a student avoid negative behavior. Answer d is incorrect because coping skills are valuable in handling stress.

120. C: Although there are many uses for intelligence tests, determining which accommodations a student accesses can help guide instruction. Intelligence testing is important in determining the intellectual abilities of students. These results can reveal how accommodations may benefit them in the classroom and which ones would be the most appropriate for them to access. Answer a is incorrect because although an intelligence test can be helpful in determining whether or not a student has an intellectual disability, this does not guide instruction. Answer b is incorrect because determining whether a student has an emotional disability would likely encompass more than just an intelligence test. Answer d is incorrect because learning disabilities are typically discovered through additional assessments as well.

121. D: Although all of these choices may be beneficial in certain situations, it would likely be a good idea to send home a brief daily summary of how the student did in class that day. It would likely be best to have the general education teachers report to the special education teacher each day about the student's positive and negative behaviors, which then would be communicated home. It is typically most effective to have just one person being the point of contact for the parents to make it more efficient. Answer a is incorrect because the student may have issues that need to be reinforced throughout the week, so this likely would not be often enough. Answer b is incorrect because it likely would not be as beneficial for the parents to be contacted multiple times throughout the day by different teachers. Answer c is incorrect because the school psychologist may or may not be able to contact the parents each day and there may be concerns or other areas that need to be communicated through the special education teacher.

122. D: Math simulation technology allows students to visualize problems that they are working on rather than just reading the text. This assistive technology can assist students with math deficiencies in conceptualizing math problems and turning them into a visual as opposed to a standard written problem. This simulation allows the students to work through the same problem as the rest of the students with a little assistance in interpreting what the problem means. Answer a is incorrect because math simulation technology does more than simply allowing the students to recognize the text. Answer b is incorrect because although it may help the students write the problems, it is designed to allow them to conceptualize each problem they are struggling with. Answer c is incorrect because math simulation is also not designed to provide opportunities for the students to hear the text.

123. C: Engaging with a student like this may prove to be the least effective strategy because it will likely make the behavior escalate. Many students are simply trying to get attention, and if they are given the attention they seek, they are going to make matters worse. It would be a better option to remain calm and possibly seek some assistance if needed. Answer a is incorrect because ignoring her behavior may cause her to stop eventually since she is not getting what she wants. Answer b is incorrect because calling for backup can be a great strategy, especially if there are safety concerns. Answer d is incorrect because removing her from class also might be the best option if the other students are being disrupted.

124. D: Although all of these choices may be beneficial for students with autism, providing hands-on instruction would likely be the best option. It is important to provide different options for students to learn, especially those students who may struggle with the content. Giving students an opportunity to learn and demonstrate their knowledge using their hands can help them to retain the information. Answer a is incorrect because it may be overwhelming for some students to give them too much information at once. Answer b is incorrect because giving a student multiple tasks might be difficult if they are struggling with the first task. Answer c is incorrect because giving students choices is sometimes a good idea, but it might be a better idea to vary the teaching methods first to see how the student learns best.

125. D: Students who receive special education services at the high school level no longer access these services when they graduate, but they can access 504 plans. These plans are designed to provide accommodations to students with disabilities in college or beyond in the workplace. Although students with disabilities cannot continue to receive these special education services when they graduate high school, it is important for them to understand the types of support that are available to them. Answer a is incorrect because students who receive special education services most often do not also have a 504 plan. Answer b is incorrect because students who exit from special education may or may not access a 504 plan, but this is not required. Answer c is incorrect because students with 504 plans are not entitled to special education services.

126. A: One of the responsibilities of paraprofessionals in many schools is to toilet students with disabilities. This will typically involve students with severe needs who are unable to toilet themselves and need additional support in this area. Although this may not always be a requirement for every paraprofessional, it is often expected as a part of the fulfillment of the duties of the job. Answer b is incorrect because it is the responsibility of the special education teacher to collaborate with the general education teachers. Answer c is incorrect because communicating with parents should also be done by the special education teacher. Answer d is incorrect because paraprofessionals are not typically involved in IEP meetings.

127. C: The constructivism theory states that learning motives are determined by the learner and by outside rewards from the community. Motivation comes not just from the learners themselves based on their knowledge but also through communicating with others. It is important to understand which approach to take when motivating students to achieve their highest potential. Answer a is incorrect because the behaviorism theory states that motivation is extrinsic. Answer b is incorrect because the cognitivism theory states that motivation for learning is intrinsic. Answer d is incorrect because the humanism theory states that motivation comes from inside the learner and is therefore intrinsic.

128. B: When working with students in small-group pull-outs, it is important that the instruction is targeted to their IEP goals. Although each student may have a different goal, the teacher must plan the lesson in a way that fits in parts of each student's goal. Students may or may not have access to the special education teacher throughout the day, so it is vital to monitor and develop these goals when working with students in small groups. Answer a is incorrect because although it is important for students to access their accommodations, they would likely access these in the general education setting. Answer c is incorrect because students do not need to access the general education curriculum when working on IEP goals in the special education setting. Answer d is incorrect because students do not need to access an alternate curriculum to work on IEP goals.

129. A: Although all of these choices may be the responsibility for students like Parker some of the time, monitoring the progress of his goals will always be the responsibility of the special education teacher. Students with learning disabilities will have academic goals that require the special education teacher to monitor them frequently. It is important for the special education teacher to monitor the goals of students to ensure that progress is being made and decide if new interventions need to be put into place. Answer b is incorrect because providing mental health support is not likely to be the responsibility of the special education teacher. Answer c is incorrect because students with learning disabilities do not always have modifications due to the impact of their disability. Answer d is incorrect because students learn learning disabilities may or may not need to access executive functioning support.

130. C: Although all of these choices may impact students throughout their lifetimes, students with multiple disabilities are likely to be impacted the most. Students with multiple disabilities have two or more disabilities that severely impact their access to education. One of these disabilities is typically an intellectual disability, which impacts students throughout their life. Answer a is incorrect because developmental disabilities impact younger students and may or may not last throughout a person's lifetime. Answer b is incorrect because students that have just speech or language impairments may end up learning to overcome these disabilities eventually. Answer d is incorrect because although specific learning disabilities may impact students in different ways, these are less likely to have an impact on a person than someone with multiple disabilities.

131. C: The prior written notice section of the IEP proposes changes that the team determines are necessary to provide FAPE for the child with a disability. The prior written notice is often the last section of the IEP, and it describes the reason for the IEP meeting and the changes that were made. Although prior written notice must be provided prior to any change in special education services, it is also included as a section in the IEP. Answer a is incorrect because a notice of meeting would be an invitation to the parents for the IEP meeting. Answer b is incorrect because providing copies of parent rights typically has a separate section in the IEP. Answer d is incorrect because a separate form must be filled out to end special education services.

132. D: Although all of these choices may provide instances to change the test or the format of the test, it is likely most beneficial to create a new test when the standards are modified. When students are unable to access the regular academic standards, it is often necessary to create a new assessment to meet the needs of these students are assess what they know. Although the majority of students can access these regular standards with accommodations or modifications, some students need to work with modified standards due to their disability. Answer a is incorrect because students who do not have access to the curriculum would likely not be assessed at all. Answer b is incorrect because students with intellectual abilities may or may not be able to access the standards with accommodations or modifications. Answer c is incorrect because accommodated tests typically do not involve a new test being created.

133. D: Although all of these strategies may be useful for Bobby in the long term, having a job is something that he is likely going to need the most. Students who are at risk and infrequently see their parents need to develop some of these independent skills sooner than other students. Because of this, they are more likely to need a job in order to be able to provide for themselves. Answer a is incorrect because students like Bobby may or may not even be thinking about going to college. Answer b is incorrect because simply giving him extra support may not help him very much in the long-term. Answer c is incorrect because although teaching him executive functioning skills may be helpful, he is more likely to need assistance in finding a job.

134. D: Although all of these choices can be beneficial in ensuring that Anna still has access to the general education curriculum in her social studies class, modifying the content can help the most with her reading comprehension struggles. Modifying the content to include less reading or fewer questions she has to answer still allows her to learn most, if not all of what her peers learn. It is important to understand how to provide support in a way that students can still learn what their general education peers are learning whenever possible. Answer a is incorrect because it may alienate Anna to move her down a grade level. Answer b is incorrect because although reteaching concepts may be beneficial, her time with the special education teacher's time may be better spent working on her reading comprehension abilities. Answer c is incorrect because a paraprofessional likely would not be as beneficial as modifying the curriculum.

135. D: Although all of these methods may be beneficial for some students more than others, including visual aids can keep students interested in the content. The use of visual aids can allow students to focus better and process the information that they are learning. It is important to engage students in the teaching process as much as possible in order to manage their attention and behavior. Answer a is incorrect because simply looking at students likely will not correct the student's behavior over time. Answer b is incorrect because simply posting the classroom rules may or may not be effective for each student. Answer c is incorrect because smiling at a student also likely will not increase positive behaviors for each student.

136. D: Although all of these choices could potentially be an issue for teachers who teach students with a wide range of needs, differentiating instruction is likely to be difficult. Differentiated instruction includes strategies to provide a curriculum that meets the needs of all of the students in the class. It can be difficult to differentiate or change the curriculum for so many students in one class in a way that meets their needs. Answer a is incorrect because IEP goals can be monitored at various times and not necessarily in one class period. Answer b is incorrect because the teacher will still need to provide the accommodations for each student. Answer c is incorrect because the teacher must still incorporate the assistive technology if a student needs it in class to access the curriculum.

137. A: Early intervention services are designed to help young children who are struggling with basic skills. Speech or communication issues are common in younger children who struggle with talking or understanding. Early intervention services are important to identify the areas that need to be targeted right away in children. Answer b is incorrect because academic services would typically come after the student has worked on early intervention skills. Answer c is incorrect because counseling services wouldn't likely begin until students were older. Answer d is incorrect because adaptive services would likely apply to older students who struggle with everyday functions.

138. C: According to IDEA, students with a dual diagnosis of a hearing and visual impairment are considered deaf-blind and receive services under that category. Students who have one diagnosis of a hearing impairment would be eligible under that category instead. It is important to under each of the areas of impact for students so they can receive all of the services they are eligible for. Answer a is incorrect because students with fluctuating hearing can still be eligible for the "hearing impairment" category. Answer b is incorrect because amplification is expected to improve a student's hearing. Answer d is incorrect because if Rob's educational performance is adversely affected by his hearing loss, he would be eligible for the category.

139. C: When teaching math to students with disabilities, many students will often learn in different ways. Because of this, it is important to incorporate different activities that include the use of senses such as touch. Incorporating some of these strategies can allow the students to learn the same content as their peers using a unique strategy that works for them. Answer a is incorrect because learning stations may not be as appropriate for math because the students are likely working on the same skill. Answer b is incorrect because interviewing students to get an idea of what they want to learn also may not be appropriate in the area of math. Answer d is incorrect because although assigning projects can be helpful in learning math, it may not be the most appropriate for fourth graders.

140. A: Students with disabilities who graduate high school will no longer be able to access their IEP from high school. This is because IDEA states that children with disabilities are only protected as long as they are attending school in the K–12 setting. These students will have access to different supports once they graduate high school. Answer b is incorrect because accommodations can still be provided when they take college classes. Answer c is incorrect because students with disabilities can always access disability services. Answer d is incorrect because accommodations must be made for individuals with disabilities in the workplace.

141. C: Although poor nutrition can certainly impact students with disabilities, this would likely be considered a physical environmental factor. Physical environmental factors impact the ways in which a student's body functions rather than their relationships and interactions with people. A person with poor nutritional habits would likely suffer illnesses to the body, which could eventually lead to a disability. Answer a is incorrect because poverty would be considered a social environmental factor because of the impact on relationships. Answer b is incorrect because the loss of a parent also impacts a person's relationships. Answer d is incorrect because family discord also is considered a social environmental factor because issues in the family can lead to damaged relationships.

142. A: According to IDEA, birth trauma would not be considered one of the causes of traumatic brain injury. Students with birth trauma would likely be considered under a different eligibility category. Students who receive services under the traumatic brain injury category will typically have a medical diagnosis of a traumatic brain injury. Answer b is incorrect because combat injuries can be one of the causes of traumatic brain injuries, even at a young age. Answer c is incorrect because violence is often associated with students who are impacted by traumatic brain injuries. Answer d is incorrect because sports-related injuries can also cause damage to the brain and cause traumatic brain injuries.

143. B: Although there are many benefits to using curriculum-based assessments, they do not always correlate to the classroom curriculum. Curriculum-based assessments are designed to monitor the progress of certain students and compare those scores to a norm. This may or may not relate to what the students are learning in class, but these measures are designed to be independent of the classroom curriculum. Answer a is incorrect because curriculum-based assessments can measure the progress of students over a short period of time such as one week. Answer c is incorrect because a teacher's instruction can be informed based on the needs of the student and what they may need to work on. Answer d is incorrect because students can chart their scores and work toward improving them.

144. B: One of the major differences between a 504 plan and an IEP is that the IEP provides services to students with disabilities. Each one of the plans provides accommodations to ensure that students with disabilities are accessing the general education curriculum. Schools must determine the impact of the disability and whether or not a service is required to provide specialized instruction. Answer a is incorrect because IEPs end after high school and 504 plans protect those with disabilities throughout their lifetime. Answer c is incorrect because 504s are governed through the Rehabilitation Act and IEPs are through IDEA. Answer d is incorrect because IEPs come from the Department of Education to protect students with disabilities, whereas 504 plans protect everyone who has a disability.

145. D: Although school psychologists may facilitate IEP meetings in certain cases, the special education teacher typically runs these meetings. The school psychologist may be involved in many phases of the meeting including assessing students and consulting with general and special education teachers. The special education teacher serves as the case manager in most instances, however, and is responsible for scheduling and running the IEP meetings. Answer a is incorrect because school psychologists will often provide mental health support to students. Answer b is incorrect because school psychologists are also often responsible for administering different kinds of tests including IQ assessments. Answer c is incorrect because school psychologists can also assist special education teachers in training staff on implementing behavior support.

146. D: Centers can be valuable strategies for students with disabilities because they can work in groups and learn from their peers. Centers provide opportunities to learn about different topics at each center group while providing opportunities to develop social skills. Students with disabilities can excel with centers because they get to work with their peers and not be responsible for an individual product. Answer a is incorrect because centers are not necessarily designed to provide instruction based on student needs and interests. Answer b is incorrect because centers do not provide individual instruction. Answer c is incorrect because centers typically provide one level of instruction for all students.

147. B: In order to allow for collaboration among students with and without disabilities, heterogeneous teams are likely to be most productive. In these groups, the teacher selects which students are in which groups in order to create a balance of ability levels among the students. This allows students with disabilities to have some success in working with students they may not always have the opportunity to work with. Answer a is incorrect because student-selected teams may leave some students with disabilities feeling left out because they were not chosen for a group. Answer c is incorrect because random teams may create an imbalance between students with and without disabilities in the class. Answer d is incorrect because homogeneous teams would group students based on ability, which would likely not make for the best balance in the class.

148. B: Screening tests can be valuable in that they provide information in determining whether or not additional assessments should be conducted. These screening tests are typically used on students who struggle in a particular area in order to determine whether or not they should be assessed further in that area. Oftentimes, screening tests can determine whether or not a special education evaluation should be conducted. Answer a is incorrect because a screening test would typically be given in order to determine whether or not a student should be evaluated for special education services. Answer c is incorrect because these screening tests cannot show progress on IEP goals. Answer d is incorrect because placement tests are typically separate from these kinds of screening tests.

149. A: One of the typical emotional developments of a preschool student is playing games with friends or others. Children of this age will often start to change the rules of a game or make up their own rules to make it more fun or interesting. Recognizing the emotions of students during these social interactions is important in determining whether or not they are developing at the expected rate. Answer b is incorrect because being rigid and not wanting to change their routine or schedule is not typical of a preschool student. Answer c is incorrect because preschool students should start to be less dependent on their caregivers. Answer d is incorrect because turn-taking is a skill that will most often develop before children enter preschool.

150. A: Although all of these choices may be effective in certain situations, tally marks would likely be most beneficial in recording the number of outbursts. Tally marks can assist the teacher in determining the number of outbursts that the student has over a period of time. These tally marks can be used to identify when or where these outbursts are occurring and how they can be prevented. Answer b is incorrect because although time sampling can be helpful for certain student behaviors, outbursts are best measured using tally marks. Answer c is incorrect because qualitative observations would describe what is happening, which may or may not provide valuable information. Answer d is incorrect because verbatim scripting would also provide qualitative information, which may or may not help the behavior.

Thank You

We at Mometrix would like to extend our heartfelt thanks to you, our friend and patron, for allowing us to play a part in your journey. It is a privilege to serve people from all walks of life who are unified in their commitment to building the best future they can for themselves.

The preparation you devote to these important testing milestones may be the most valuable educational opportunity you have for making a real difference in your life. We encourage you to put your heart into it—that feeling of succeeding, overcoming, and yes, conquering will be well worth the hours you've invested.

We want to hear your story, your struggles and your successes, and if you see any opportunities for us to improve our materials so we can help others even more effectively in the future, please share that with us as well. **The team at Mometrix would be absolutely thrilled to hear from you!** So please, send us an email (support@mometrix.com) and let's stay in touch.

If you feel as though you need additional help, please check out the other resources we offer:

Study Guide: http://mometrixstudyguides.com/CEOE

Flashcards: http://mometrixflashcards.com/CEOE